W9-BRV-113

THE PROHIBITION ERA

ALEXANDER GRAHAM BELL
AND THE TELEPHONE

THE ATTACK ON PEARL HARBOR

THE CALIFORNIA GOLD RUSH

THE CIVIL RIGHTS ACT OF 1964

THE ELECTRIC LIGHT

THE LOUISIANA PURCHASE

THE MONROE DOCTRINE

THE OUTBREAK OF THE CIVIL WAR

THE PROHIBITION ERA

THE ROBBER BARONS AND
THE SHERMAN ANTITRUST ACT

THE SINKING OF THE USS *MAINE*

SPUTNIK/EXPLORER I

THE STOCK MARKET CRASH OF 1929

THE TRANSCONTINENTAL RAILROAD

THE TREATY OF PARIS

THE WRIGHT BROTHERS

THE PROHIBITION ERA

TEMPERANCE IN THE UNITED STATES

LOUISE CHIPLEY SLAVICEK

The Prohibition Era

For information, contact:

Chelsea House
An imprint of Infobase Publishing
132 West 31st Street
New York, NY 10001

Library of Congress Cataloging-in-Publication Data

Slavicek, Louise Chipley, 1956-
The prohibition era : temperance in the United States / by Louise Chipley Slavicek.
p. cm. — (Milestones in American history)
Includes bibliographical references and index.
ISBN 978-1-60413-005-8 (hardcover)
1. Prohibition—United States—History. 2. Temperance—United States—History.
I. Title. II. Series.
HV5089.S58 2008
363.4'1097309042—dc22 2008024150

Chelsea House books are available at special discounts when purchased in bulk quantities for businesses, associations, institutions, or sales promotions. Please call our Special Sales Department in New York at (212) 967-8800 or (800) 322-8755.

You can find Chelsea House on the World Wide Web at http://www.chelseahouse.com

Text design by Erik Lindstrom
Cover design by Ben Peterson
Composition by North Market Street Graphics, Inc.
Cover printed by Yurchak Printing, Landisville, PA
Book printed and bound by Yurchak Printing, Landisville, PA
Date printed: November, 2011
Printed in the United States of America

This book is printed on acid-free paper.

Contents

The Prohibition Era: America Goes Dry

At 12:01 A.M. on Saturday, January 17, 1920, the United States of America became a dry nation. For the next 12 years, 10 months, and 18 days until its repeal on December 5, 1933, the Eighteenth Amendment to the Constitution prohibited Americans from manufacturing, selling, or transporting alcoholic beverages. Tens of thousands of distilleries, breweries, and saloons across the country were compelled to close their doors as the United States embarked on one of the most colorful and controversial periods in its history: the Prohibition Era.

On the evening of January 16, 1920, with the official start of national Prohibition just hours away, exultant "drys" (those who supported the ban on alcohol) assembled in churches and auditoriums across the country to commemorate the triumph of a cause for which many had fought tirelessly over the years. In Washington, D.C., a huge victory rally drew hundreds of dry lawmakers, representatives from the country's two most powerful anti-liquor organizations (the Anti-Saloon League and the Women's Christian Temperance Union), and scores of well-wishers. Alcohol had been part of the everyday fabric of Americans' lives since colonial times, yet during the century leading up to Prohibition, many in the country became convinced that alcohol consumption imperiled the physical and emotional health of drinkers and resulted in squandered wages, lost work time, increased violence, and splintered families. Consequently, in January 1920, Prohibition supporters looked forward confidently to a bright new era for American society, one characterized by lower rates of crime, divorce, and poverty, as well as enhanced productivity.

On the eve of the country's experiment with legally mandated sobriety, not everyone celebrated. At restaurants and saloons throughout the United States, thousands of drinkers mourned the demise of their right to drink. Some held mock wakes for John Barleycorn, a traditional symbol for alcoholic beverages. In New York City, reputedly America's "wettest" city, one popular watering hole gave its patrons tiny wooden caskets as mementos. At a lavish farewell party in the Park Avenue Hotel, guests dressed in black filed solemnly past a large coffin filled with black liquor bottles. As it turned out, however, wets had far less reason to mourn and drys to celebrate than either group could have imagined on the night of January 16.

Although most scholars agree that per-capita alcohol consumption among Americans of drinking age declined during the Prohibition Era, tens of millions of people, including an unprecedented number of women, drank alcohol regularly throughout the period. Indeed, the Eighteenth Amendment and its enforcing legislation, the Volstead Act, may have been the most widely and flagrantly disobeyed federal laws in U.S. history. Despite Prohibitionist hopes that drinking in the United States would die out quickly after January 1920, the nation's 13-year dry spell inspired normally law-abiding wets

The National Prohibition Convention of 1892 took place in Cincinnati, Ohio. The Prohibition Party, which was founded in 1869, sought to prohibit the consumption of alcoholic beverages.

to defy the new prohibitory statutes by any means possible. They concocted bathtub gin; made home-fermented beer and wine in their kitchens, basements, and bathrooms; and hounded their doctors for prescriptions for medicinal liquor. In 1929 alone, U.S. pharmacists filled 11 million prescriptions for whiskey.

Particularly in the country's larger cities, defiant drinkers frequented clandestine bars called speakeasies, where they guzzled bootleg (illegally obtained) liquor smuggled in from abroad, manufactured in illegal stills, or pilfered from legal stocks of medicinal or industrial alcohol. By the mid 1920s, much of this booming underground liquor industry had fallen under the control of mobsters like Chicago's infamous Al Capone, who made millions from his various bootlegging enterprises before he was imprisoned for tax evasion in 1931.

By 1930, rampant flouting of the nation's anti-alcohol statutes had caused a majority of Americans, including many teetotalers (people who abstain from drinking), to conclude

This is a tombstone dedicated to John Barleycorn, giving his death as January 16, 1920, the date that the Eighteenth Amendment went into effect in the United States. Barleycorn is a character from an English folksong who personifies grain barley and the alcohol that can be made from it.

that Prohibition was fundamentally unenforceable and ought to be repealed. The Great Depression (the severe economic downturn that started with the stock market crash of October 1929 and lasted through the 1930s) only served to reinforce pro-repeal sentiment in the United States. A revitalized alcohol industry would bring desperately needed new jobs and tax revenue to the country's faltering economy, many Americans believed, and government funds spent on Prohibition enforcement could be redirected to assist the hungry and homeless.

With the election of pro-repeal Democrat Franklin D. Roosevelt as president in November 1932, it was clear that the nation's dry days were numbered. On December 5, 1933, the Prohibition Era officially came to a close, when the Twenty-first Amendment, which invalidated the Eighteenth Amendment and re-legalized the sale and production of liquor, was ratified by a three-quarters majority of the states.

Not surprisingly, Prohibition's champions and its critics viewed the fundamental purpose and merit of the experiment with constitutional sobriety very differently. For its supporters, state-mandated temperance was a means of uplifting American society through promoting greater economic productivity, family stability, and personal virtue. For its detractors, though, Prohibition represented an unconscionable assault on individual rights by an intrusive and narrow-minded government. Regardless of one's particular perspective on Prohibition's actual intent and worth, however, this much is indisputable: By demonstrating the tremendous difficulties involved in enforcing governmental restrictions on private behavior, the Prohibition Era has profoundly influenced U.S. political life, up to and including the present. Not since the repeal of the Eighteenth Amendment has the federal government sought to control the personal morals of Americans to such a degree as during the 13 turbulent years of the Prohibition Era.

Prohibition's Roots

By 1919, when the Eighteenth Amendment was ratified, drinking alcoholic beverages had been part of everyday American life for more than three centuries. From the founding of the first English settlements in Virginia and Massachusetts in the early 1600s, imbibing was a central facet of the American colonial experience. Colonists, influenced by traditional Old World attitudes, viewed alcohol not as a luxury, but rather as "a necessity to be kept close at hand," according to historians Mark Lender and James Martin.[1]

DRINKING IN COLONIAL AMERICA: BEER AND HARD CIDER

In homes across colonial America, including Puritan New England, beer and hard, or alcoholic, cider were the customary beverages at mealtime for grownups and children alike.

Milk, because it was highly perishable, was usually made into butter and cheese. Tea and coffee, which were too expensive for most colonists' budgets, did not become popular in North America until well into the 1700s. Water was generally viewed as unhealthful, so it was not consumed regularly. This was an attitude that the settlers carried with them from the Old World, where most lakes, streams, and rivers were too polluted to be a safe source of drinking water.

Consumption of alcoholic beverages was also widespread outside of the home during the colonial era. Farmers and craftsmen alike enjoyed a glass of beer during regular mid-morning and mid-afternoon work breaks. Social and community gatherings inevitably featured alcohol at such events as weddings, militia musters, barn raisings, election days, and even funerals and ordinations. In 1678, mourners at a funeral reception for Mary Norton, the wife of one of Boston's most prominent ministers, reportedly guzzled more than 50 gallons (189 liters) of costly imported wine. Several years later, in nearby Woburn, Massachusetts, guests at an ordination ceremony for the Reverend Edwin Jackson downed 25 gallons (95 liters) of wine, 4 gallons (15 liters) of rum, 2 gallons (7.6 liters) of brandy, and almost 7 barrels of hard cider.

Many male colonists also drank regularly at public houses, or taverns, although female customers were barred by tradition from public houses. Taverns were a fixture in almost every community in the late 1600s, and large towns like Boston boasted dozens of public houses. In addition to food, a convenient place for political and other public meetings, and lodging for travelers, public houses offered a wide range of alcoholic refreshments, including distilled liquor like rum, whiskey, and gin, as well as the usual beer and cider.

Although it was a common and accepted practice in early America to drink alcohol, it was not acceptable to drink to the point of drunkenness; in fact, drunkeness was considered a serious threat to the good order of the community. Throughout the colonies, civil authorities punished drunkards with fines, whippings, or imprisonment. Church authorities also frowned upon bingeing, which they condemned as ungodly, as well as irresponsible, behavior. The leading Puritan divine (religious leader), Increase Mather, declared that drunkenness was "a brutish sin" that deeply offended the Almighty.[2] Communities that permitted their members to drink intemperately, Mather warned, risked heavenly retribution in the form of pestilence, famine, drought, or some other misfortune.

WHISKEY AND BINGEING: CHANGING DRINKING PATTERNS AFTER THE REVOLUTION

The disapproval of the church leadership and the community in general, combined with the threat of legal penalties, helped keep excessive drinking to a minimum in colonial America, at least in public places. During the decades after the Revolutionary War (1775–1781), however, Americans began to consume larger quantities of alcohol than ever before. According to some estimates, per-capita consumption of alcohol by 1820 among those 15 years of age or older had risen from an average of 5.8 gallons (22 liters) to more than 7 gallons (26.5 liters), a level that would remain fairly stable for the next two decades. Historians have linked America's shifting drinking patterns during the late eighteenth and early nineteenth centuries to two new economic and social developments: the greater availability and affordability of whiskey, and the weakening of traditional community checks on individual drinking habits.

Imported rum was popular in many coastal communities during the colonial era, but until the late eighteenth century, the vast majority of Americans consumed their alcohol in the form of beer and hard cider. Typically, these naturally fermented beverages had alcohol contents of no more than 4 to 7 percent. Whiskey, gin, and other distilled liquors, which have alcohol contents of 40 to 50 percent, were generally more expensive and difficult to obtain than beer and cider. The disparity between the cost and availability of fermented (rather than distilled) alcohol began to change, however, as Americans moved farther inland, crossing the Appalachian Mountains and moving into the fertile expanses of the Ohio Territory and the southern frontier.

The settlers quickly discovered that they could grow more grain on their new farms than they could consume. As they sought markets for their surplus crops in the more densely populated East, they realized that it was easier and cheaper to transport their rye, corn, and barley to market in the form of whiskey rather than as food, which was bulkier and more perishable than liquor. Consequently, whiskey became more plentiful and less expensive than it had ever been in North America, which caused many Americans to give up their traditional beer and cider for the more potent liquor.

According to historians, as a result of the unprecedented availability and affordability of whiskey, many white American males condoned drinking to the point of drunkenness. It was still widely considered inappropriate for respectable white females to drink heavily. African Americans of both sexes also rarely drank to the point of inebriation. At the time, the vast majority of blacks in America were enslaved, and most slaveowners forbade heavy drinking among their slaves, fearing that drunkenness would lead to lost work time, vandalism, or violence.

From the late 1700s through the 1830s, however, white men were significantly more likely to binge, alone or in a group, than ever before in American history. In addition to the unprecedented supply of whiskey, some scholars have linked the upsurge in bingeing to a new emphasis on individual liberty and social equality after the Revolutionary War. The ideals of personal freedom and egalitarianism, these historians argued, tended to undermine the influence of traditional community norms and the opinions of one's social "betters," such as church and civil authorities, on all sorts of individual behavior, including drinking.

BENJAMIN RUSH SOUNDS THE ALARM REGARDING "SPIRITUOUS" LIQUOR

One of the first Americans to call attention to the post-Revolutionary shift in drinking preferences and practices was also one of the nation's most prominent citizens, Dr. Benjamin Rush. A signer of the Declaration of Independence, former surgeon general of the Continental Army, and the author of dozens of medical publications, Rush was the most well-known physician of his time in America. The unprecedented popularity of whiskey after the Revolutionary War, as well as the rise in bingeing that went along with it, deeply dismayed the Philadelphia doctor. Determined to alert the American public to what he considered a dangerous new trend in the nation's drinking habits, Rush published a groundbreaking tract in 1784 that condemned the use of whiskey and other distilled or "spirituous" liquors.

Entitled *An Inquiry into the Effects of Spirituous Liquors upon the Human Body, and Their Influence upon the Happiness of Society*, Rush's treatise decisively contradicted long-held beliefs that alcohol had health-promoting properties—beliefs Americans had inherited directly from their European ancestors. Alcoholic beverages of all kinds, it was generally thought, helped to ward off fevers, soothe overworked muscles, and warm the blood in cold weather. Most people agreed, however, that distilled liquor was by far the most therapeutic of the various forms of alcohol. Since the colonial days, noted author John Kobler, American physicians had routinely prescribed spirits "for practically every affliction from painful teething in infancy to the aches of old age."[3]

In sharp contrast to the traditional American faith in hard liquor's exceptional medicinal value, Rush argued in his *Inquiry*

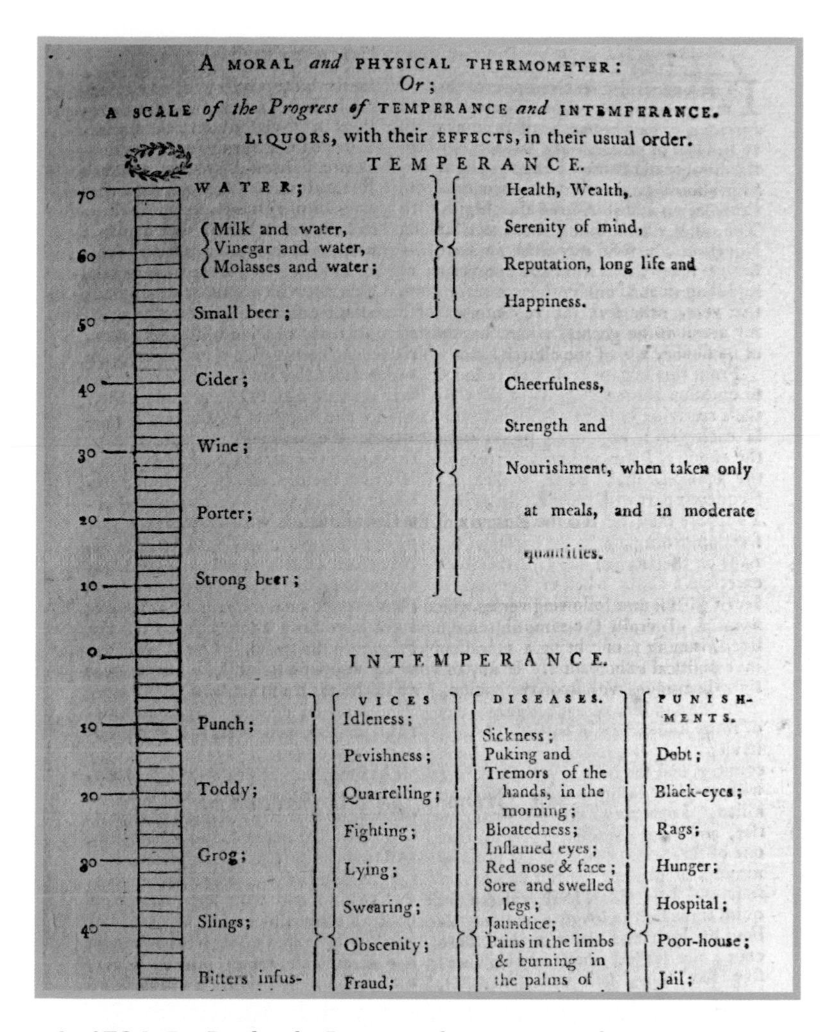

A MORAL *and* PHYSICAL THERMOMETER:
Or;
A SCALE *of the Progress of* TEMPERANCE *and* INTEMPERANCE.
LIQUORS, with their EFFECTS, in their usual order.

TEMPERANCE.

70 WATER; — Health, Wealth,

60 Milk and water, Vinegar and water, Molasses and water; — Serenity of mind, Reputation, long life and Happiness.

50 Small beer;

40 Cider; — Cheerfulness,

30 Wine; — Strength and Nourishment, when taken only

20 Porter; — at meals, and in moderate quantities.

10 Strong beer;

0

INTEMPERANCE.

		VICES	DISEASES.	PUNISHMENTS.
10	Punch;	Idleness;	Sickness;	Debt;
		Peevishness;	Puking and Tremors of the hands, in the morning;	
20	Toddy;	Quarrelling;		Black-eyes;
		Fighting;	Bloatedness;	Rags;
30	Grog;	Lying;	Inflamed eyes; Red nose & face;	Hunger;
		Swearing;	Sore and swelled legs;	Hospital;
40	Slings;	Obscenity;	Jaundice; Pains in the limbs & burning in the palms of	Poor-house;
	Bitters infus-	Fraud;		Jail;

In 1784, Dr. Benjamin Rush published a tract that condemned the use of whiskey and other distilled liquors, setting the temperance movement in motion. Part of Rush's work included this "Moral and Physical Thermometer," which rates beverages based on their supposed healthful or ill effects.

that, although lighter alcoholic beverages such as wine were wholesome when drunk in moderation, spirits were invariably hazardous to the health. By overstimulating the body's nervous system, Rush maintained, spirituous liquors promoted "every form of acute disease" from diabetes to "liver obstruction" to epilepsy.[4] Moreover, he argued, strong drink was so habit forming—both mentally and physically—that anyone who indulged in distilled alcohol risked becoming addicted.

Rush was not only concerned about the effects of distilled liquor on drinkers' physical and mental well-being. He also worried about its impact on their moral character and political judgment. Like many of his compatriots, Rush was convinced that the survival of the young American Republic rested on a virtuous and informed citizenry. "Intemperate [i.e., willing to consume alcohol] and corrupted voters" posed a grave danger to the Republic, he warned, because such men could not be depended on to choose wise, morally upright leaders over smooth-talking demagogues.[5]

THE TEMPERANCE MOVEMENT TAKES OFF

Rush wanted to ensure that the *Inquiry* reached the widest possible audience, so until his death in 1813, he regularly updated his treatise and oversaw the distribution of thousands of copies of the tract's various editions to religious and political leaders across the nation. Widely quoted in newspapers, state assemblies, town halls, churches, and institutions of higher learning, Rush's diatribe against hard liquor played a critical role in sparking America's first organized temperance activity. Within two years of the *Inquiry's* initial printing in 1784, the Quaker churches of New England had ordered their members to stop drinking distilled alcohol altogether. In 1789, America's first known temperance society was founded in Litchfield County, Connecticut, by a group of prominent farmers and merchants.

Inspired by Rush's well-publicized crusade against spirituous liquor, dozens of small temperance associations formed throughout the United States in the beginning of the nineteenth century. Yet it was not until a decade after the physician's death, during the so-called Age of Reform, that anti-liquor activism become a true mass movement in the United States.

Lasting from approximately the early 1820s to the mid 1850s, the Age of Reform was characterized by an intense and widespread interest in social and moral reform, especially among middle-class Americans.

Historians agree that anxiety about the far-reaching changes in American society and culture during the first half of the 1800s, including industrialization, urbanization, and mounting immigration, crime, and poverty rates, helped spur the nation's newfound passion for reform. In an era of economic and social upheaval, many Americans worried that traditional ethics and religious values were being forgotten or shoved aside. Using a wide range of reform activities to improve public education, rehabilitate criminals, abolish slavery, and eradicate intemperance and profanity, they sought to direct their quickly changing society back onto what they considered the right moral track.

During the Age of Reform, religion played a key role in motivating and emboldening temperance workers and other reformers. This was especially true of the evangelical Christianity of the Second Great Awakening, a series of Protestant revivals that swept the country during the early 1800s. The crusading and profoundly optimistic Christianity of the Second Great Awakening emphasized that believers had the power to transform their troubled nation into the perfect godly community, a beacon of holiness in a dark and corrupt world. Inspired by the lofty principles of revivalism, temperance reformers devoted themselves to curing Americans of their "sinful" drinking habits as a first step toward building the ideal Christian society.

The evangelicals' hopeful expectations for their homeland are evident in the anti-liquor sermons and tracts of the leading temperance reformer and evangelist Reverend Lyman Beecher. Beecher once described intemperance as "a national sin carrying destruction from the center to every extremity of the empire."[6] Nevertheless, he was supremely confident that pious Americans could banish drunkenness from their country, setting a moral and spiritual example for others to follow: "Our nation has been raised up by Providence to exert an efficient instrumentality in this work of moral renovation," he declared in 1826. "Who can doubt that the spark which our forefathers struck will yet enlighten the entire continent?"[7]

FROM TEMPERANCE TO PROHIBITION

Driven both by anxiety over the economic and social changes sweeping their nation and an optimistic faith in the perfectibility of American society, temperance reformers formed thousands of voluntary associations between the mid 1820s and early 1830s with a combined membership of more than a million persons. Most of these groups were affiliated with America's first national temperance organization, the American Temperance Society (ATS).

Founded in Boston in 1826 by evangelical Protestants, the ATS quickly became the largest and best-funded temperance association at the time in America. The Society published reams of anti-liquor tracts, sermons, and essays, and it sent volunteer and paid lecturers all over the country to preach the evils of intemperance. The ATS's top strategist, as well as one of its most effective speakers, was Reverend Justin Edwards. Like other ATS lecturers, Edwards had a dramatic and frequently accusatory style. One of the minister's favorite targets was liquor merchants, whom he angrily denounced as heartless villains: "Over every grog [liquor] shop ought to be written in great capitals, THE ROAD TO HELL, LEADING DOWN TO THE CHAMBERS OF DEATH," Edwards thundered. "You sell to the healthy, and you poison them. . . . That is abominable, and ought to receive universal execration."[8]

The ATS did not attack lower-proof alcoholic beverages at first. By the late 1830s, however, in common with many other American temperance groups, it had moved beyond renouncing just hard liquor and embraced teetotalism—which is total abstinence from all types of beverage alcohol, including beer and wine. Spearheaded by the American Temperance Union (ATU), a national umbrella organization founded in 1836, the drive to make the United States a dry, or nondrinking, nation at first relied entirely on moral persuasion. The ATU at first tried to convince individuals to abstain voluntarily through education and example; by the 1840s however, the ATU and many other temperance associations had decided that a more coercive approach to the nation's drinking problem was needed. They believed that prohibition—outlawing the manufacture and sale of liquor—was the only way to eliminate the blight of alcohol from American society once and for all.

Historians have suggested that a sharp upsurge in the number of German and Irish immigrants to the United States during the mid-nineteenth century contributed to the anti-liquor movement's new attempts to use the law to force teetotalism on Americans. Temperance reformers were deeply troubled by the flood of German and Irish immigrants that entered the United States during the 1840s and 1850s, because of the role that drinking played in their native cultures. They were shocked that, on the Sabbath, the Germans visited taverns or beer gardens, which were boisterous, open-air establishments where families and friends socialized and downed tankards of beer. The drinking habits of the Irish newcomers, the majority of whom were young males who had fled the Irish potato famine, disturbed dry activists even more. Already wary of their Catholic religion and poverty, temperance workers were dismayed by the popularity of bingeing among the Irish immigrants, who seemed to equate heavy drinking with manliness.

THE CHANGING FORTUNES OF THE PROHIBITION MOVEMENT

Despite the concerns of the dry reformers about alcohol-guzzling immigrants, per-capita consumption of hard liquor by Americans aged 15 and older actually fell between 1830

(continues on page 18)

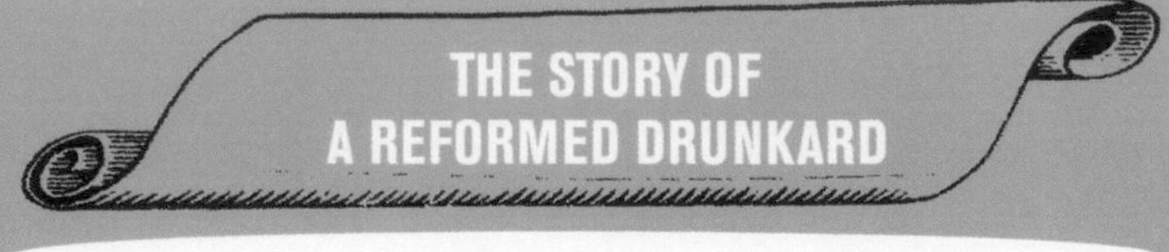

THE STORY OF A REFORMED DRUNKARD

One of best-known and most popular of the early nineteenth century temperance orators was John Henry Willis Hawkins (1797–1858) of Baltimore, Maryland. Hawkins began to drink heavily at the tender age of 14 when he was serving as an apprentice to a hatter who, like many other American employers of the period, promised his workers daily rations of hard liquor in return for their diligence on the job. Despite his heavy drinking, Hawkins managed to establish himself as a hatter, marry, and start a family during his twenties.

By the time Hawkins was his early forties, however, his drinking had developed into full-blown alcoholism, and his life, both professional and personal, was a shambles. In June 1840, Hannah, Hawkins's beloved younger daughter, finally convinced him to give up alcohol for good after a 14-day-long drinking binge. That same year, he helped found the Washington Temperance Society, the first anti-liquor organization that consisted entirely of reformed drunkards. Recruited by the Washingtonians to give talks on his own battle with alcoholism, Hawkins quickly discovered he had a talent as a public speaker. From the early 1840s until his death in 1858, he gave thousands of lectures in towns and cities all over the United States on the terrible toll alcohol had taken on his own and his loved ones' lives. In the following excerpts from one of his published temperance speeches, Hawkins dramatically describes how he finally freed himself from his addiction to alcohol, and he calls on his listeners to join him in embracing sobriety:

> During the first two weeks of June [1840] I drank dreadfully, bought liquor by the gallon and drank and drank. I cannot tell

how I suffered: in body every thing, but in mind more! By the fourteenth of the month—drunk all the time—I was a wonder to myself, astonished that I had any mind left; and yet it seemed, in the goodness of God, uncommonly clear. My conscience drove me to madness. I hated the darkness of the night, and when morning came I hated the light, I hated myself, hated existence. . . . I asked myself, "Can I restrain [from drinking]? Is it possible?" But there was no one to take me by the hand and say ***you can.*** I had a pint of whisky in my room, where I lay in bed, and thought I would drink it, but this seemed to be a turning point for me. I knew it was life or death as I decided to drink it or not. . . .

Then my daughter Hannah, came up—my only friend, I always loved her the most—and she said, "Father, don't send me after whisky today!" I was tormented before; this was agony. I could not stand it, so I told her to leave, and she went downstairs crying, and saying, "Father is angry with me." My wife came up and asked me to take some coffee. I told her I did not want anything of her and covered myself up in bed. Pretty soon I heard someone in the room, and, peeping out, I saw it was my daughter.

"Hannah," said I, "I am not angry with you—and—***I shall not drink any more.***" Then we wept together. . . . Poor drunkard! There is hope for you. You cannot be worse off than I was, no more degraded or more of a slave to appetite. You can reform if you will. ***Try it! Try it!****

---

*Quoted in Kobler, *Ardent Spirits,* pp. 60–61.

(continued from page 15)

and 1845, from 7 gallons (26.5 liters) to 2 gallons (7.6 liters), according to some estimates. Temperance groups, and especially the two national anti-liquor organizations, the ATS and its successor, the ATU, deserve much of the credit for this impressive decline. During the early 1850s, the anti-liquor campaign achieved even greater success when lobbying pressure by the ATU and other groups helped persuade more than a dozen state legislatures to adopt statewide prohibitory laws. In 1851, Maine became the first state to ban the sale and production of alcohol except for medicinal purposes. By 1855, 13 other midwestern and northeastern states and territories, including Massachusetts, Rhode Island, Connecticut, Vermont, New Hampshire, Delaware, New York, Indiana, Ohio, Michigan, Iowa, Illinois, and the Minnesota territory, had followed Maine's example and passed similar laws.

Yet most of the anti-liquor movement's impressive legislative victories during the early 1850s were to prove fleeting. As the bitter sectional conflict between North and South intensified during the second half of the decade, the nation's attention was diverted away from social and moral reform movements like temperance. By 1860, four of the dry states had repealed their prohibitory laws, and in most of the remaining ones, enforcement of anti-liquor legislation was spotty at best. During the Civil War (1861–1865) and the turbulent Reconstruction era that followed, almost all of the 14 states and territories that had adopted Prohibition during the 1850s rescinded or significantly weakened their anti-liquor laws.

In 1869, hoping to revive their troubled cause, temperance enthusiasts founded a national political organization, the Prohibition Party, and began to field candidates for local and national offices. Nationally and even regionally, the Prohibition Party proved unable to compete effectively with the powerful Republican and Democratic parties. By the early 1870s, the discouraging performance of the Prohibition Party at the polls, combined with the repeal or weakening of the statewide prohibitory laws passed during the 1850s, had caused many Americans to conclude that liquor reform was a lost cause. Then, in 1873, something unexpected happened. The struggling campaign against alcohol suddenly gained a new lease on life with an entirely new kind of dry movement: the Women's Crusade, the first female-led offensive on drinking in U.S. history.

The Prohibition Movement Gains Momentum

By 1870, it was beginning to look as though the American public had permanently lost interest in the temperance movement. Then, in late 1873, the long fight to reform the nation's drinking habits suddenly entered an exciting new phase ushered in by the Women's Crusade, in which American women confronted the liquor trade.

It was hardly surprising that women should assume a central role in the faltering anti-liquor movement. According to the conventional wisdom of the era, women were naturally more virtuous, pious, and family oriented than men. As a result of this supposed moral, spiritual, and domestic superiority, women had a sacred responsibility to defend the very foundation of American society—the family—against such corrupting influences as profanity, gambling, licentiousness, and, last but not least, intemperance. Protection of home and hearth against

Unidentified men stand at the bar of a popular saloon in New York City around 1905. One reason that so many women joined the temperance cause was that they were often subjected to the ills that followed the reckless drinking of men.

irresponsible male drinking was vitally important, female temperance enthusiasts believed, because drunkards all too often undermined the stability of their families and communities by neglecting, abusing, or abandoning their wives and children.

THE WOMEN'S CRUSADE AND THE WCTU

The opening battle in the Women's Crusade against alcohol took place in December 1873 in the small, middle-class community of Hillsboro, Ohio, shortly after a charismatic temperance lecturer named Diocletian Lewis visited town. Lewis's dramatic account of how his long-suffering mother prayed her alcoholic husband's favorite tavern right out of business thrilled his female listeners. One day, pushed to her limits by her husband's constant bingeing, Lewis related, the usually timid Mrs. Lewis decided to fight back. Directly outside the bar where her husband did most of his drinking, she began to pray loudly for the saloon's misguided owner. Finally, after Mrs. Lewis prayed and read Scripture for hours, the mortified barkeeper agreed to close the doors of his establishment permanently. Inspired by this story of the heroic Mrs. Lewis, several dozen Hillsboro women vowed to hold prayer and Bible reading vigils in front of their community's saloons and other establishments that sold alcohol. Soon the determined women had pressured several local liquor dealers to shut down.

As word of the Hillsboro "pray-ins" spread in early 1874, women across the nation enthusiastically adopted the crusaders' direct action approach to the alcohol problem. Within a few months, Bible-toting female picketers had managed to put hundreds of saloons and breweries out of business. Despite its promising beginnings, however, the Women's Crusade proved short-lived. In an era when women were expected to stay close to home and submit to men in all things, the crusaders' willingness to take to the streets and directly challenge male liquor vendors shocked and fascinated the American public. Consequently, the Crusade at first attracted an enormous amount of free publicity from newspapers around the nation. By the autumn of 1874, media and public interest in the campaign were already starting to wane, and many of the liquor establishments that had been prayed shut had quietly reopened.

In November 1874, just as the Women's Crusade was losing momentum, the female war on alcohol was reenergized by the founding of a nationwide Prohibition group composed exclusively of women in Cleveland, Ohio. Under the direction of

This 1874 *Harper's Weekly* illustration shows women crusaders pleading with a saloonkeeper to stop serving alcohol.

the forceful and highly educated Frances Willard, the Women's Christian Temperance Union (WCTU) deliberately distanced itself from the sensational tactics of the Women's Crusade. Instead, Willard and the WCTU focused on lobbying; they demanded that local elementary schools include mandatory anti-drink courses in their curriculums and ask state legislators to pass prohibitory laws. Convinced that America would never free itself from alcohol's evil snare until women won the vote and could help put Prohibition candidates in office, Willard also closely aligned her organization with the growing women's suffrage movement in the United States. Since males were naturally more susceptible to liquor's temptations than women, she insisted, only "the mothers and daughters of America" could be entrusted to vote consistently for Prohibition measures.[1]

(continues on page 26)

CARRY NATION
(1846–1911)

Temperance Activist

The best-known female temperance activist and one of the most colorful figures in American history was Carry A. Nation. Born Carry Amelia Moore on November 25, 1846, Nation grew up on a Kentucky plantation. Mental illness ran in Carry's family: Her mother believed she was Queen Victoria of England, and she drove through the Kentucky countryside in a gilt carriage, waving haughtily to her bemused neighbors.

The Civil War ruined Carry's slave-owning father financially, and he moved his family west to Missouri in 1865. There, 19-year-old Carry fell in love with Charles Gloyd, a doctor and Civil War veteran. The couple married in 1867, but the union was short-lived. Charles turned out to be an alcoholic and after Carry became pregnant, she decided it would be in her own and the baby's best interests if she moved back home with her parents. When Gloyd died at the age of 29 in 1869, Carry blamed his early death entirely on his drinking.

In 1877, Carry married David Nation, a preacher, lawyer, and strict teetotaler. Twelve years later, the couple moved to Medicine Lodge, Kansas, where Nation, inspired both by her deep religious convictions and her tragic first marriage, soon became active in the local chapter of the Women's Christian Temperance Union (WCTU). Nation was incensed that Medicine Lodge harbored several saloons, even though in 1880 Kansas had become the first state since the Civil War to prohibit the sale and manufacture of alcoholic beverages. Breaking with the tactics of the WCTU, Nation adopted the direct action approach of the old Women's Crusade of the 1870s and began to sing hymns and pray aloud at the doors of the illegal bars.

By the late 1890s, Nation was convinced that her peaceful tactics were not working and decided to adopt more a more aggressive approach in her anti-drink crusade. Armed with rocks, bricks, and empty bottles, the six-foot (1.83 meters) tall, 175-pound (79.38

kilograms) Nation began to storm illegal saloons all over Kansas, gleefully smashing bars and their contents to smithereens. In January 1901, Nation used a hatchet in her saloon-wrecking campaign for the first time, and the small, short-handled axe soon became her trademark. Nation's decidedly unladylike exploits brought her international notoriety; over the next decade, backed by a small group of female supporters, she staged a series of highly publicized hatchet assaults on saloons all over the country, from California to Washington, D.C.

Although some temperance supporters viewed Nation as a heroine, the WCTU leadership was clearly embarrassed by her antics and tried to distance itself from her. "She has a method all her own, and one which is not found in the plan of the work of the W.C.T.U.," an editorial in the organization's newspaper noted, concluding that "more harm than good must always result from lawless methods."*

To support herself and pay the fines she incurred as a result of her saloon invasions, Nation turned to the lecture circuit during the early 1900s. She billed herself as "Carry A. Nation," because she hoped that her anti-drink crusade would carry the nation to sobriety. In January 1911, Nation, whose health had been failing for some time, made what would be her last temperance speech in Eureka Springs, Arkansas. "I have done what I could," she told her audience before she collapsed on stage. On June 2, 1911, Nation died in a Kansas hospital at the age of 64. In accordance with her wishes, she was buried near her parents' graves in Missouri, beneath a marker that proclaimed, "Faithful to the Cause of Prohibition/'She Hath Done What She Could.' "**

---

*Quoted in Burns, *The Spirits of America,* p. 143
**Ibid., p. 146.

(continued from page 23)

THE REVEREND HOWARD RUSSELL FOUNDS A NEW KIND OF ANTI-LIQUOR ORGANIZATION

Despite Frances Willard's belief in the critical importance of women to the success of the anti-drink movement, the single most important organization in securing national Prohibition would be an all-male group launched a few years before the WCTU leader's death in 1898: the Anti-Saloon League. The Anti-Saloon League's founder, the Reverend Howard Russell, was a man with a powerful sense of mission: He believed God had personally called him to save his home state of Ohio from the scourge of intemperance.

The Congregationalist minister and longtime teetotaler first became aware of the Almighty's plan for him one spring day when he was taking a stroll and found himself passing directly in front of a crowded saloon. Bowing his head in prayer, he pled with the Almighty to "stay the tide of sin and shame flowing therefrom." Suddenly, Russell related, he heard God's voice speak to him quite plainly: "You know how to do it; go and help answer your own prayers," the Lord commanded.[2] On May 24, 1893, soon after he received this heavenly summons, Russell officially founded the Ohio Anti-Saloon League, although God, the Reverend liked to say, was the League's true Creator.

From the beginning, Russell sought to link his new organization to those evangelical Protestant denominations that had traditionally preached temperance. Yet despite its close ties to evangelical Protestantism, the Anti-Saloon League (ASL) was by far the most business-oriented and politically shrewd anti-liquor group in the history of the temperance movement. According to historian Thomas Pegram, Russell, who had been a Republican politician and successful attorney before he entered the ministry, deliberately fashioned

> the League's organizational structure so as to duplicate the centralization, bureaucracy and efficiency of a business.

This print, issued by A.D. Fillmore in 1855, expounds on the evils of alcohol. In the center grows a gnarled tree whose roots are schnapps, whiskey, wine, beer, and other spirits. Around its trunk winds a giant serpent with an apple in its mouth and a mug of beer on its head. The trunk branches out into limbs marked "Diseases Corporeal," "Ignorance," "Vice," "Crime," and "Immorality." These in turn divide into smaller branches representing a plethora of social and moral evils, such as wars, drunkenness, anarchy, counterfeiting, dueling, and "Breach of the Peace."

> Although representatives of churches and other temperance groups sat on ASL boards, actual control of operations at the state and national levels rested in the hands of salaried superintendents and their professional staffs. Superintendents determined strategy, wrote model bills, fashioned publicity, lobbied legislators, managed fund-raising, and orchestrated the protests and pleas of the League's . . . following.[3]

By the end of 1893, the League's professional and highly disciplined approach had inspired temperance supporters in nine states and the District of Columbia to form similar groups. On December 18, 1895, these various associations merged to become the American Anti-Saloon League, with Russell as the organization's first general superintendent.

"THE SALOON MUST GO!"

The motto of the new American Anti-Saloon League—"The Saloon Must Go"—reflected a central conviction of late nineteenth century anti-liquor activists. During the last decades of the 1800s, the number of saloons multiplied throughout the United States, particularly in the nation's expanding urban areas. By 1900, there were an estimated 300,000 saloons in the nation, most of them in the large cities of the Northeast and Midwest. Some boasted posh decors and an elite, well-heeled clientele, but these upper-class watering spots were the exceptions to the rule. Most saloons served a much less prosperous clientele and were anything but elegant. Indeed, many of them were seedy, smoke-filled dives.

Despite their often shabby appearance, saloons were important and highly valued institutions in many lower-income communities, especially in the urban neighborhoods where they were most common. Urban saloons were convenient places for male community members (females were typically excluded) to hold labor union, charitable, and political meetings, discuss important community issues, or connect with potential employers, as well as to relax over a glass of beer or whiskey. "In the nineteenth and early twentieth centuries," writes Edward Behr, "the saloon was not only the one place working-class men . . . got together and socialized, but it also served as their only available employment agency and club. There were newspapers, mailboxes, pencils, paper, bulletin boards advertising jobs, card tables and sometimes bowling alleys and billiard tables."[4] The typical urban saloon charged nothing for these amenities and conveniences. "It asked only for the regular and continued patronage of its customers," according to historian Michael Lerner.[5]

So great was its hostility toward the saloon, however, that the Anti-Saloon League completely disregarded any economic and social benefits neighborhood bars might provide to their chiefly working- and lower-class customers. As far as the Leaguers were concerned, all saloons were dangerous and corrupt institutions that tempted men to neglect their families and served as magnets for society's least desirable elements, including drunkards, gamblers, hoodlums, prostitutes, and corrupt politicians who plied patrons with free alcohol in return for their votes. Saloons, they were convinced, were a blight on the community and had to go, for the sake of their misguided customers as well as the Republic as a whole.

AN AMBITIOUS AGENDA AND A PRAGMATIC APPROACH

Yet despite its name and chief slogan, the Anti-Saloon League hoped to accomplish a great deal more than merely eliminating saloons from the American landscape. Russell and the other Leaguers did not only want the saloon to go, notes author Eric Burns: "they wanted everything to go, not just rum shops of tawdry atmosphere, but *all* rum shops, in addition to *all* breweries, *all* distilleries, *all* vineyards, and, as a consequence, *all* customers and their horrible, unceasing thirsts."[6]

To fulfill their ambitious goal to destroy America's liquor traffic, the ASL focused on two major political objectives: to secure new anti-alcohol legislation on the local and state levels and obtain better enforcement of existing prohibitory laws. The first step to achieve these aims, League officials concurred, was to get more dry politicians elected. Despite the Prohibition Party's fervent commitment to make America a dry nation, the ASL was hesitant to align itself too closely with that organization. Wary of the Prohibition Party's consistently dismal showings at the polls, the pragmatic Leaguers preferred instead to work within America's traditional two-party system. Whether a candidate happened to be a Democrat or Republican was of no importance to the ASL, notwithstanding the Republican leanings of Russell and most of the rest of its directors. All that mattered was that, once in office, a politician could be counted on to back stricter anti-liquor laws.

Wherever success appeared likely, the ASL pushed for statewide prohibitory laws. In those states that balked at going bone dry, the organization was more than willing to make political compromises to ease the way to prohibition. The League fought for the passage of local-option laws in states with strong pockets of wet or pro-drink voters, instead of focusing on statewide political contests. Local-option laws allowed relatively small groups of voters the opportunity to prohibit the manufacture and sale of alcohol within particular counties, incorporated towns and villages, townships, municipalities, or even city precincts. As fragmentary as local-option victories might appear, the ASL's pragmatic strategists viewed local-option laws as a way to conquer an entire state for Prohibition, one county, town, or city ward at a time. "The Leaguers fought with the patience of driver ants," writes John Kobler: "They fought a war of attrition. No community was too small, no proposed prohibitory measure too trivial to merit their attention."[7]

LABORING FOR THE CAUSE: FUND RAISING AND PROPAGANDIZING

Dry-leaning Democratic and Republican candidates soon discovered that having the nonpartisan ASL on their side was usually a big advantage. "The league proved that it could marshal votes for anyone—Republican or Democratic," according to Mark Lender and James Martin.[8] It was not only votes that cooperation with the ASL guaranteed, Democratic and Republican campaign managers soon learned, but also money, and lots of it.

One of the things that "the Anti-Saloon League did best," notes Eric Burns, "was raise money, more money than temperance had ever raised before."[9] The WCTU, a close ally of the ASL by the late 1890s, chipped in, but churches were the ASL's most important source of funds. The League worked diligently to persuade ministers from traditionally dry evangelical Protestant denominations to lend their pulpits to ASL representatives to mobilize dry voters, as well as to solicit donations, a process that one superintendent bluntly called "prying open the churches."[10] The League made a point of sending its most forceful and charismatic speakers to the churches they managed to "pry open," and when the lecturers invariably concluded their orations by passing around the collection plate, most congregations responded generously, so generously that by 1900 the ASL boasted a yearly budget of $2 million.

Reflecting its leadership's deep faith in the power of the printed word, the League used most of the substantial money that it raised each year to produce campaign literature designed to win votes for dry candidates and discredit their wet opponents. By 1909, the ASL was publishing such a tremendous volume of anti-liquor propaganda that the organization decided to found the American Issue Printing Company, its own printing plant in Westerville, Ohio. American Issue rapidly established itself as the nation's largest temperance publisher, and it churned out millions of leaflets, flyers, and posters that plugged particular candidates or pieces of legislation, as well as daily, weekly, and monthly newspapers, a quarterly magazine, and a yearbook. Its numerous periodicals provided ASL members with the latest Prohibition news, as well as compelling moral, medical, and political arguments to use when trying to convert others to the dry cause.

RURAL PROTESTANTS AND URBAN PROGRESSIVES: THE ASL AND PROHIBITION'S POPULAR BASE

The ASL's generously funded, professionally organized, and politically savvy anti-liquor campaign was to prove remarkably effective. In 1906, just one decade after the League's creation, more than one-third of the American population, or about 35 million people, resided in communities that had outlawed the sale and manufacture of liquor, and local-option laws were in force in 30 different states. During the final years of the 1800s and first years of the 1900s, most of the popular support for the ASL and prohibition came from two very different groups: the first was concentrated in the nation's rural communities and the second in its burgeoning urban centers.

Between the founding of the ASL and the outbreak of World War I in 1914, the transformation of the United States accelerated dramatically. What had been a predominantly agricultural, rural, and Anglo-Saxon Protestant nation before the Civil War became an industrialized, largely urban, and ethnically and religiously diverse one. These sweeping changes alarmed the ASL's numerous rural supporters; they were especially worried about the swelling urban immigrant population, which in addition to the usual German and Irish drinkers included millions of wine-drinking and beer-guzzling newcomers from the "wet" cultures of southern and eastern Europe. America's swiftly expanding cities, they fretted, would become hotbeds of alcohol-fueled crime and depravity, and imperil the moral core of the entire nation. For the League's conservative rural backers, Prohibition represented a chance to impose their traditional evangelical

Carry A. Nation is shown here, holding a hatchet and a bible, around 1900. After losing her first husband to alcoholism, Nation embarked on a colorful saloon-wrecking crusade that would make her the most famous temperance activist in American history.

Protestant values on their wayward urban neighbors and put the United States back on what they viewed as the right spiritual and moral path.

The Anti-Saloon League's second major source of popular support during the late 1800s and early 1900s was a loosely knit coalition of reformers known as the Progressives. Typically middle- or upper-class city dwellers trained in law, medicine, teaching, social work, or business, Progressives hoped to use their expertise to create a more humane and just society. Although more liberal and secular in outlook than Prohibition's rural backers, Progressives shared their concerns regarding the rapid growth of the cities and the waves of impoverished immigrants who were fueling that growth. Before they were allowed to get any worse, the Progressives believed, the government must tackle the expanding cities' many problems, including spiraling crime, unsanitary housing, corrupt political bosses, and last but not least, what one reformer described as "the free-and-easy drinking customs" of their exploding ethnic populations.[11]

Progressives were convinced that excessive alcohol consumption, although not the sole cause of rising urban poverty and crime rates, contributed enormously to these social ills. Consequently, a key element of the Progressive reform program was to pressure the state to enforce sobriety among all economic classes of Americans through outlawing, or at least severely restricting, the manufacture and sale of liquor.

During the late nineteenth and early twentieth centuries, as in the tumultuous Age of Reform era of the early 1800s, Americans struggling to adapt to rapid economic and social change again turned alcohol into a powerful public issue. By 1913, popular support for Prohibition, especially among evangelical rural and Progressive urban voters, had grown to the point that fully half of the nation's citizens, or about 45 million people, lived in states, counties, or cities that forbade the manufacture and sale of alcohol. In February of that same year, the ASL achieved its most important political victory to date when it successfully lobbied members of the U.S. Congress to pass the first major national dry law, the Webb-Kenyon Act, banning the shipment of alcohol from wet to dry states. After two decades of struggling for liquor reform at the state and local levels, anti-liquor activists were finally ready to turn their attention to realizing what had once seemed an all but impossible dream: national Prohibition.

The Battle for a Prohibition Amendment

A national ban on alcohol, and not merely the extension of dry territory under local-option or state laws, had always been the Anti-Saloon League's ultimate aim. The League did not begin to believe its ambitious goal was truly within its reach, however, until the winter of 1913, when Congress approved the first significant national anti-liquor law, the Webb-Kenyon Act, which prohibited the transport of alcoholic beverages into dry states.

ASL officials announced their intention to make America a dry nation in November 1913 at their Jubilee Convention in Columbus, Ohio, which marked the League's twentieth anniversary. Former Indiana governor James Hanley, the convention's keynote speaker, told 5,000 League members that they would achieve this lofty objective through an amendment to the U.S. Constitution. In the document's 125-year history, it had been amended only 17 times before. When Hanley proclaimed that the new amendment "shall forever prohibit throughout the territory of the United States the manufacture and sale and the importation, exportation and transportation of intoxicating liquor," loud cheers and applause filled the auditorium.[1]

On a cold December morning a few weeks later, several thousand League members, Women's Christian Temperance Union members, and other anti-liquor activists assembled in front of the White House to show their support for an amendment to the Constitution. Carrying long banners inscribed "NATIONAL CONSTITUTIONAL PROHIBITION" and singing temperance songs, the Prohibitionists paraded down Pennsylvania Avenue to the U.S. Capitol Building. On the Capitol's east steps, the general superintendent of the ASL, Purley Baker, shook hands with Representative Richmond Hobson of Alabama and Senator Morris Sheppard of Texas, two of Congress's most zealous drys. Then Baker formally presented the legislators with a proposal for an Eighteenth Amendment to the Constitution drafted by League officials. Prohibition was critical to the very survival of the American Republic, the resolution dramatically asserted, because alcohol "lowers to an appalling degree the average standard of character of our citizenship, . . . produces widespread crime, pauperism and insanity, [and] inflicts disease and untimely death upon hundreds of thousands of citizens."[2]

FASHIONING A DRY CONGRESS: WAYNE WHEELER AND THE ASL GO TO WORK

It is no easy task to amend the U.S. Constitution, as the Anti-Saloon League and their prohibitionist allies hoped to do. First, the proposed amendment would need to be approved by a two-thirds majority in both houses of Congress, a far more difficult task than securing the simple majority (more than 50 percent) required to pass other bills. Then, for the amendment to go into effect, fully three-quarters of the states had to ratify it, either by a simple majority vote in their various legislatures or in special statewide conventions.

Although Hobson and Sheppard promptly introduced the resolution to their respective legislative bodies, it ended up stalled in the House and Senate Judiciary Committees, which would determine the constitutionality of the proposed amendment. The resolution's slow progress through the Judiciary Committees did not worry ASL officials; in fact, they viewed it as something of a godsend. Given the current makeup of Congress, League strategists realized, when the bill did come up for vote it was extremely unlikely to win a two-thirds majority in either chamber. With this in mind, in early 1914, the ASL launched an energetic and well-funded campaign to return as many reliably dry legislators to Capitol Hill as possible in the upcoming November elections.

In 1914, the Anti-Saloon League put Wayne Wheeler, one of the organization's most powerful and effective officials, in charge of getting more Prohibition-friendly politicians into the Senate and House. Wheeler, who had been recruited to serve as the organization's chief legal adviser in 1898 by the League's founder, Howard Russell, was utterly committed to the dry cause and the ASL's pragmatic, nonpartisan approach. Although a firm Republican himself, Wheeler helped engineer the defeat of Ohio's defiantly wet Republican governor in 1905 by his Democratic opponent. As a behind-the-scenes political manipulator and lobbyist, Wheeler, or the "Dry Boss," as he was nicknamed, reputedly had no equal, and under his sway the League would become "the most influential pressure group of its day," write Lender and Martin.[3]

Wheeler was determined to mobilize all of the League's considerable human and material resources behind dry candidates in every corner of the nation. Between January and November 1914, he sent tens of thousands of ASL speakers and other campaign workers, both salaried professionals and volunteers, "into every Congressional district where there was

Wayne Bidwell Wheeler was instrumental in persuading the states to ratify a Prohibition amendment. Nicknamed the "Dry Boss," Wheeler was a master lobbyist and behind-the-scenes political manipulator who was utterly committed to the dry cause.

a chance to elect a dry and waged as strong a fight as candidates have ever seen," he later boasted.[4] The Dry Boss also devoted considerable time and energy toward lobbying congressional incumbents to support the amendment.

In addition to personal visits, Wheeler sought to win over wavering legislators by bombarding them with letters and telegrams from ASL members, as well as from other pro-amendment voters back home. To drum up popular support for the ASL's congressional letter-writing campaign and for dry candidates throughout the country, Wheeler depended heavily on the League's own American Issue Publishing Company. During the final few months before the November elections, the American Issue presses ran continuously, spewing out ten tons of campaign and anti-drink literature daily. All in all, the League spent a record $2.5 million in 1914 to rally support throughout the country for the constitutional amendment and the dry cause generally.

PROHIBITION'S FRIENDS AND FOES IN THE BUSINESS WORLD

When the League began its crusade for national Prohibition, as had been true ever since the ASL's founding, the organization's rank-and-file, middle-class membership was its most important source of funds. Yet, by 1914, the Anti-Saloon League was also receiving substantial sums of money from a wealthy and elite group of American financiers and industrialists, including Henry Ford, Andrew Carnegie, Cyrus McCormick, and John D. Rockefeller, among others.

Self-interest appears to have been the chief motivating factor for Ford and the other business magnates who donated to the ASL during the early 1900s. They believed that in a modern, technological society, employees who drank were a threat not only to workplace safety but also to productivity. By the 1910s, Henry Ford, creator of the famous Model T automobile and pioneer of the moving assembly line, had become one of the ASL's largest benefactors. Ford was so convinced of the harmful effects of alcohol on his workers' efficiency—and therefore his own profits—that he pledged to fire any employee caught drinking alcohol, even in the privacy of his own home. To ensure that his factory workers remained abstinent 24 hours a day, Ford maintained a large staff of private detectives to spy on them. Other business owners also tried to restrict their employees' drinking outside as well as inside the workplace, although few went so far as to fire workers caught drinking on their own time.

At the same time that the ASL was winning valuable allies like Henry Ford in the business community, it was making some formidable enemies in the brewing and distilling industries, whose leadership was naturally dismayed by the expanding Prohibition movement. "For the first time in American business history," writes historian K. Austin Kerr, "two sizeable industries faced extinction, without any financial compensation, as a result of the deliberate efforts of a reform movement."[5] In an effort to counter the League's increasing political influence throughout the country during the first years of the twentieth century, brewers and distillers published reams of anti-Prohibition literature, made generous campaign donations to wet candidates, and lobbied state and local officeholders to vote against dry laws.

Yet despite some early successes in local and state political contests, the liquor industry's defense against prohibition was faltering by 1914. American distillers and brewers had long been bitter commercial rivals, but by the mid-1910s, that rivalry had reached new heights. Beer, which could now be produced in greater volumes as a result of improved brewing technologies, surpassed distilled alcohol as America's favorite alcoholic beverage.

Just as the ASL's new constitutional amendment campaign was making the need for unity and cooperation within the drink trade more critical than ever, the soaring popularity of beer, particularly among the country's large urban population, had convinced many brewers that their product was safe from the Prohibitionists. Because Americans could never be persuaded to give up their beer, the brewers optimistically believed, the Prohibitionists would be compelled to settle for an amendment that outlawed only hard liquor. The amendment crusade, they reasoned, was the distillers' problem, not theirs, and consequently they were not willing to devote large amounts of their time or funds to fight it. As the brewers would soon discover, they had gravely underestimated the strength, determination, and cunning of the ASL and its prohibitionist allies.

A DRY CONGRESS AND A WORLD WAR

The election results of November 1914 greatly encouraged the ASL's leadership. For the first time, drys outnumbered wets in the Senate. Dry legislators also picked up a number of seats in the House of Representatives, although not enough to win the two-thirds majority necessary to send a constitutional amendment to the states for ratification. Determined to bring more drys to Washington in the next general election in 1916, ASL activists "laid down such a barrage as candidates for Congress had never seen before, and such as they will, in all likelihood, not see again for years to come," Wayne Wheeler later recalled with pride.[6] In November, the League's energetic campaigning was rewarded when voters sent twice as many prohibition candidates as wets to the House. Congressional approval of the proposed Prohibition amendment now seemed all but guaranteed.

On April 6, 1917, before the amendment bill had a chance to come up for a vote in the newly dry House and Senate, Congress declared war on Germany, and the United States entered World War I on the Allied side. For nearly three years since the conflict of the Central Powers (primarily Germany, Austria-Hungary, and Turkey) against the Allies (chiefly Great Britain, France, and Russia) first erupted in Europe, President Woodrow Wilson had adamantly refused to involve the United States in the fighting. In the wake of a series of German submarine attacks on passenger and merchant vessels in the Atlantic that claimed dozens of U.S. lives, however, the president and Congress, with the strong backing of most of the American public, decided the nation could no longer remain neutral.

Anti-Saloon League officials immediately realized that U.S. entry into the war had given them a powerful new weapon in their ongoing battle to make America sober: patriotism. From the start, Leaguers made a concerted effort to link the dry cause as intimately as possible to America's war effort. In keeping with this strategy, Wheeler helped secure congressional backing for the Lever Food and Fuel Control Act, a wartime measure designed to conserve vital fuel and food supplies, during the summer of 1917. What made the bill so attractive to the League was that it promised to halt, or at least drastically decrease, wartime production of spirits by authorizing President Wilson to divert grain from the distilled liquor industry. The League used slogans such as "Shall the many have food, or the few have drink" and "Save 11,000,000 Loaves a Day," to rally public opinion behind the Lever Act and against the "liquor traffic" by portraying distillers as squanderers of precious grain that could be used to feed the troops.[7]

The Anti-Saloon League viewed the war as an excellent opportunity to discredit the booming brewing industry, as well as the hard liquor trade. To that end, Leaguers shamelessly played on the growing anti-German sentiment within the United States after April 1917. Once Congress formally declared war on Germany, Wheeler and his ASL associates quickly pointed out that the vast majority of the country's brewers were of German heritage. Moreover, they noted, German Americans were closely tied to the saloon business, because breweries had taken control of many the nation's bars in recent years, particularly in urban areas.

At the League's insistence, in February 1918, Congress launched an investigation of the leading ethnic German organization in the United States, the German-American Alliance, for allegedly unpatriotic activities. The Alliance, which counted numerous brewers among its 2 million members, was an outspoken foe of Prohibition, as well as a vocal champion of Germany in its struggle against the Allies. Although the Congressional investigation failed to turn up any evidence of treasonous activities by the Alliance, in the midst of all the negative publicity generated by the probe the organization disbanded, thereby depriving the brewing industry of one of its most loyal supporters.

VICTORY

By December 1917, the prohibition proposal had finally made its way through both chambers of Congress. Given the large number of drys voted into Congress in 1916, no one was surprised when the resolution easily won the two-thirds majority required for approval, with the Senate voting 62 to 20 and the House 282 to 128 in favor of the new amendment. Nevertheless, Prohibition activists figured that it was bound to be a more difficult and drawn-out process to get 36 states—a three-quarters majority—to ratify the amendment.

At the time that the amendment proposal passed Congress, 26 of the nation's 48 states had already enacted prohibitory laws. Yet as the Prohibitionists well knew, these laws varied widely in their severity, and only 13 of the supposedly dry states completely outlawed the sale, manufacture, or importation of alcoholic beverages within their borders. In Virginia, for example, males over the age of 18 who were not currently enrolled in college could buy as much as three gallons (11.36 liters) of beer, one gallon (3.79 liters) of wine, or one quart (.95 liters) of hard liquor per month. In Alabama, liquor could not be manufactured or sold within the state, but adult citizens were permitted to import two quarts (1.89 liters) of spirits, two gallons (7.57 liters) of wine, or five gallons (18.93 liters) of beer from wet states every other week. In stark contrast to these lenient state laws, the proposed constitutional amendment banned the manufacture, sale, or transportation of all intoxicating liquors from or to any location within the United States or its territories.

Despite the fact that only a little over one-quarter of the states were actually bone dry as of December 1917, however, the Prohibition Amendment moved rapidly through the ratification process. Within 12 months of its approval by Congress, 15 state legislatures had endorsed the new amendment and, in January 1919, the pace picked up, with 20 states ratifying within the first two weeks of the new year. On January 16, a little more than two months after a cease-fire agreement between Germany and the Allied Powers ended World War I, Nebraska became the thirty-sixth state to endorse national Prohibition, securing the required three-quarters majority. Ultimately, only 2 of the 48 states—Connecticut and Rhode Island—declined to ratify. "No previous amendment," note Lender and Martin, "had ever passed so quickly and with so clear a mandate from the states."[8] A century of anti-liquor activism and 25 years of expert lobbying by the Anti-Saloon League, wartime restrictions on distilled liquor and prejudice against German American brewers, and an inequitable distribution of legislative seats between rural and urban areas that allowed rural—and therefore, dry—domination of most state legislatures, all contributed to the remarkably swift ratification of the Eighteenth Amendment.

The Eighteenth Amendment decreed a 12-month grace period from final ratification until the law went into effect, with January 17, 1920, designated as the date for national Prohibition to begin. Except for the rather vague statement that "the Congress and the several States shall have concurrent power to enforce this article by appropriate legislation," however, the amendment failed to address the critical issue of how the government intended to ensure compliance with the new law beginning in January 1920. To strengthen the amendment,

(continues on page 48)

After several months of debate, on October 10, 1919, the House of Representatives adopted the Volstead Act by an overwhelming majority of 321 to 70 votes. When the bill reached President Wilson's desk, however, he promptly vetoed it on constitutional grounds. "In all matters having to do with personal habits and customs of large numbers of our people, we must be certain that the established processes of legal change are followed," Wilson declared.* "I am in favor of local option," he further explained: "I am a thorough believer in local self-government."**

The dry-dominated Congress was so committed to the stringent law that, on October 28, just one day after receiving word of Wilson's action, legislators were easily able to muster the two-thirds majority needed to override the presidential veto. They scheduled the Volstead Act to take effect a little less than three months later on January 17, 1920, the same day that the Eighteenth Amendment was slated to take effect. The following excerpts are from the Volstead Act, Title II: Prohibition of Intoxicating Beverages:

SEC. 3. No person shall on or after the date when the Eighteenth Amendment to the Constitution of the United States goes into effect, manufacture, sell, barter, transport, import, export, deliver, furnish or possess any intoxicating liquor except as authorized in this Act, and all the provisions of this shall be liberally construed to the end that the use of intoxicating liquor as a beverage may be prevented. Liquor for nonbeverage purposes and wine for sacramental purposes may be manufactured, purchased, sold, bartered, transported, imported, exported, delivered furnished and possessed, but only as herein provided. . . .

SEC. 7. No one but a physician holding a permit to prescribe liquor shall issue any prescription for liquor. And no physician shall prescribe liquor unless after careful physical examination of

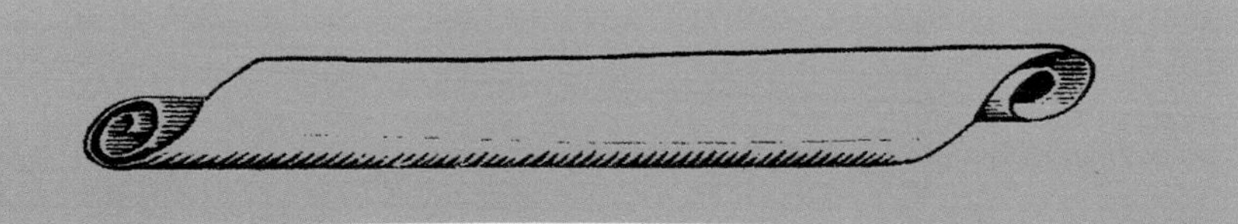

the person for whose use such prescription is sought, or if such examination is found impracticable, then upon the best information obtainable, he in good faith believes that the use of such liquor as a medicine by such person is necessary and will afford relief to him from some known ailment. Not more than a pint of spiritous liquor to be taken internally shall be prescribed for use by the same person within any period of ten days and no prescription shall be filled more than once. . . .

SEC. 18. It shall be unlawful to advertise, manufacture, sell, or possess for sale any utensil, contrivance, machine, preparation, compound, tablet, substance, formula direction, recipe advertised, designed, or intended for use in the unlawful manufacture of intoxicating liquor. . . .

SEC. 21. Any room, house, building, boat, vehicle, structure, or place where intoxicating liquor is manufactured, sold, kept, or bartered in violation of this title, and all intoxicating liquor and property kept and used in maintaining the same, is hereby declared to be a common nuisance, and any person who maintains such a common nuisance shall be guilty of a misdemeanor and upon conviction thereof shall be fined not more than $1,000 or be imprisoned for not more than one year, or both. . . .

SEC. 29. Any person who manufactures or sells liquor in violation of this title shall for a first offense be fined not more than $1,000, or imprisoned not exceeding six months, and for a second or subsequent offense shall be fined not less than $200 nor more than $2,000 and be imprisoned not less than one month nor more than five years.

Any person violating the provisions of any permit, or who makes any false record, report, or affidavit required by this title, or violates

(continues)

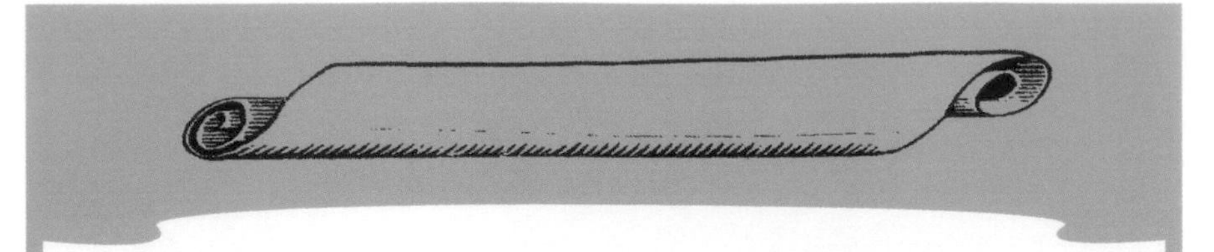

(continued)

any of the provisions of this title, for which offense a special penalty is not prescribed, shall be fined for a first offense not more than $500; for a second offense not less than $100 nor more than $1,000, or be imprisoned not more than ninety days; for any subsequent offense he shall be fined not less than $500 and be imprisoned not less than three months nor more than two years. . . .

*Quoted in Behr, *Prohibition,* p. 78.
**Quoted in Burns, *Spirits of America,* p. 184.

(continued from page 45)
in October 1919, Congress passed the National Prohibition Act, which was written almost entirely by Wayne Wheeler. Despite Wheeler's authorship, the enforcement statute soon came to be known as the Volstead Act, after its sponsor in the House of Representatives, Congressman Andrew Volstead of Minnesota.

The Volstead Act, although highly restrictive in most regards, did include several important exclusions regarding the commercial manufacture and distribution of alcohol. First, the Act authorized the manufacture of denatured industrial alcohol, an indispensable product in the nation's growing chemistry industry. (Denatured alcohol is alcohol that has been made unfit for consumption, generally by adding poisonous substances.) Second, it allowed the use of existing stocks of wine for Christian and Jewish religious observances and distilled liquor for medicinal purposes. Finally, the Act permitted the manufacture and sale of a very weak form of beer known as near beer, with an alcohol content of one-half of one percent or lower. This last provision brought scant comfort to American brewers, however; right up until the last minute most had clung to the hope that regular beer, with its relatively low alcohol content of between 3.5 and 6 percent, would be exempt from the new prohibitory laws.

In addition to defining what was permissible and what was not after the Eighteenth Amendment went into effect, the Volstead Act also established penalties for violators. Any person caught brewing, distilling, selling, or transporting illegal alcohol was subject to a $1,000 fine and six months in prison for the first offense, and up to a five-year jail term and $2,000 fine for the second offense. The Act assigned responsibility for enforcement to the commissioner of the Internal Revenue Service, who organized his Prohibition agents into the Prohibition Unit (later renamed the Prohibition Bureau). Prohibition agents were given broad powers to fight the illegal liquor trade, including the authority to padlock shut any building in which illegal alcoholic beverages were sold or manufactured for one year and to confiscate and auction off cars, boats, and other personal property used to transport illicit liquor. With the approval of the stringent Volstead Act and the creation of the Prohibition Unit, anti-liquor activists eagerly anticipated the birth of what they were confident would be a sober America on January 17, 1920.

Defying the Ban: Moonshine and Speakeasies

On January 16, 1920, just hours before Prohibition became the law of the land, America's best-known itinerant evangelist, former professional baseball player Billy Sunday, celebrated by holding a mock funeral for John Barleycorn, an imaginary figure that represented whiskey and other alcoholic beverages. "Good-bye, John! You were God's worst enemy. You were hell's best friend," Sunday, a recovered alcoholic and ardent Prohibitionist, intoned over Barleycorn's coffin at the Norfolk, Virginia, church where he had been leading a revival for the past few days. "The reign of tears is over," the evangelist promised the thousands of dries who had jammed into the tabernacle to witness the symbolic burial of America's hard-drinking past. "The slums will soon be a memory. We will turn our prisons into factories and our jails into storehouses and corncribs. Men will walk upright now, women will smile, and children will laugh," Sunday joyfully predicted.[1]

Despite Sunday's boundless optimism regarding the social, physical, and spiritual benefits Prohibition would soon bring to American society, the anti-liquor forces' seemingly decisive victory in January 1920 turned out to be a hollow one. Although most Americans either stopped or at least decreased their consumption of alcoholic beverages from 1920 until 1933, when the Eighteenth Amendment was repealed, a sizable minority did not. Indeed, no sooner had the Volstead Act gone into effect than Americans began to dream up ways to get around the restrictive legislation.

Historians can only speculate regarding how many Americans drank illegally for the 13 years that national Prohibition lasted. What scholars can say with some certainty, however, is that most of the drinking that occurred during the Prohibition Era took place in America's rapidly growing urban areas. Generally speaking, men and women who resided in rural villages and small towns were far more likely to comply with the new anti-liquor legislation than their big city neighbors. The nation's more conservative and ethnically homogenous backcountry and small-town communities "contained the bulk of Women's Christian Temperance Union and Anti-Saloon League members. Also concentrated there were many of the one-third to two-fifths of American adults who had not used alcohol before prohibition and a substantial number of those who gave up drinking when liquor became illegal," observes historian David Kyvig. "Prohibition violation," he concludes, "occurred most frequently in large cities from San Francisco to New Orleans to New York."[2]

HOME DISTILLING: ALKY COOKERS AND BATHTUB GIN

According to the Volstead Act, it was illegal to make, sell, or transport beverages with an alcoholic content greater than 0.5 percent. It was not illegal, however, to drink intoxicating beverages of any strength within the privacy of one's own home or as a bona fide guest in a friend's home. Wayne Wheeler was dismayed by the personal-use exemption, but the more moderate voices in Congress had refused to vote for the Volstead Act in 1919 without it. Congressional moderates also added a provision to the Act that banned Prohibition agents from searching private dwellings unless they had clear evidence that illegal alcohol had been sold there.

Encouraged by these major loopholes in the Act, wets stocked up on their favorite alcoholic beverages during the months and weeks before national Prohibition went into effect, stashing bottles in basements, closets, garages, and storage sheds. Yet only an elite minority of Americans had enough disposable income to buy up large quantities of alcohol. Consequently, after January 16, 1920, millions of normally law-abiding citizens, particularly in the nation's urban areas, decided to quench their thirsts by making their own alcoholic beverages.

Many Prohibition Era do-it-yourselfers experimented with distilling hard liquor at home, which was generally perceived as requiring less skill than brewing beer or fermenting wine at home. Indeed, it was common knowledge among most Americans that small-time country distillers had been furtively cooking up illegally distilled corn whiskey, called moonshine or hooch, in simple, makeshift stills to sell to their backcountry neighbors for years to avoid government licensing requirements and liquor taxes.

It was not difficult for most of Prohibition's amateur distillers to obtain the necessary equipment to distill raw alcohol in their own basements, kitchens, or bathrooms. Cash-strapped do-it-yourselfers could fashion a makeshift "alky cooker" from a copper kettle, a coffee percolator, a washtub, or even a trash can. Thousands of other fledgling distillers invested in more sophisticated but relatively inexpensive store-bought stills. During the early 1920s, hardware stores in cities and larger

Federal agents inspect illegal stills during Prohibition. In 1930, Prohibition agents seized nearly 300,000 stills.

towns across the nation sold portable, one-gallon (3.79-liter) copper alky cookers for just six dollars.

Because the Volstead Act forbade the sale of intoxicating beverages but not the equipment that could be used to make those beverages at home, storeowners stocked up on the popular home stills, displaying them openly. Eric Burns believes that Wayne Wheeler, the legislation's chief author, ignored the issue of home distilling when he wrote the Volstead Act because he believed Americans would rather drink nothing at all than settle for low-quality whiskey. Wheeler, a teetotaler, could not have been more mistaken. Emboldened by the Volstead Act's ban on residential searches, during the 13 years that Prohibition remained the law of the land, countless died-in-the-wool wets throughout the nation distilled and drank their own homemade foul-tasting, throat-searing booze.

Most of the ingredients needed to make homemade spirits were as readily available to amateur distillers as the equipment in which the illegal whiskey was cooked and distilled. Fledgling distillers soon discovered that, when cooked with yeast and water, almost any kind of sugar—whether from apples, bananas, or other fruits; cereal grains; or even potato peelings—could be distilled into a potent alcoholic beverage. Corn sugar, which was readily available at most urban grocery stores, seems to have been particularly popular with home distillers: Between 1919 and 1930, sales of corn sugar mash increased sixfold in the United States.

The pure, 200-proof alcohol that do-it-yourselfers distilled from fermented corn or other types of sugar mash was too concentrated to drink safely. Consequently, after stirring in a few drops of a flavoring agent such as juniper oil, which imparted a gin-like taste, home distillers filled their bottles or jugs no more than half full of alcohol, then topped off the potent concoction with water. According to David Kyvic, the juniper-flavored "bathtub gin," one of the most popular homemade liquors of the Prohibition Era, got its unusual name because the bottles or jugs into which the ersatz gin was typically poured were too tall to fit under a sink tap but not under a bathtub tap. Hence, when home distillers topped off their phony gin with water, "the process was usually carried out in the bathtub," notes Kyvic.[3]

MALTING AND FERMENTING: DO-IT-YOURSELF BEER AND WINE

Although making homemade beer required more finesse, equipment, and ingredients than cooking whiskey, home brewing appears to have been nearly as common as home distilling in the Prohibition Era. During America's 13-year dry spell, "the air became thick with new kinds of industrial fumes; it was on some occasions possible for a person to walk an entire town or city block, if not more, without ever losing the scent of brew from the residences he passed," writes Eric Burns. "It could hardly have been otherwise," he observes: "People were malting, mashing, boiling, hopping, fermenting, siphoning, settling—all the things that a professional brewer might do, but amateurishly."[4]

Because America's novice beer makers lacked the training and more sophisticated equipment of the professional brewer, their brew usually bore only a faint resemblance to the popular commercially produced beverages of pre-Prohibition days. According to contemporary standards, homemade brew all too often had a sour, yeasty smell, muddy appearance, and bitter taste that reminded many of laundry soap. As for the effect of the homemade beer, one do-it-yourselfer complained: "After I've had a couple of glasses I'm terribly sleepy. Sometimes my eyes don't seem to focus and my head aches. I'm not intoxicated, understand, I merely feel as if I've been drawn through a knothole."[5]

Despite the generally abysmal quality of home brew, however, grocery and hardware stores continued to do a brisk business selling canned malt syrup, hops, yeast, rubber tubing, bottles, capping machines, and other beer-making ingredients and paraphernalia throughout the twenties. By mid-decade, annual sales of home-brewing supplies averaged an impressive $136 million, and in 1926 and 1927, "the national production of malt syrup . . . came close to 888,000,000 pounds [403.6 million kilograms]," notes author John Kobler: "Allowing a normal 10 percent for non-brewing uses, enough remained for 6.5 billion pints [3.08 billion liters] of beer."[6]

Before January 1920, the vast majority of American drinkers favored beer and hard liquor over wine, but during the Prohibition Era, home fermentation of wine grew rapidly in popularity. Certain immigrant groups in the United States, particularly those from southern and eastern Europe, had a long tradition of making their own wine. After national Prohibition went into effect, Americans from all ethnic backgrounds, including many who had never been regular wine drinkers, decided to try to make the fermented drink.

America's new wine-making craze was directly related to an obscure provision of the Volstead Act. Apparently motivated by a desire to keep the nation's burgeoning grape-growing industry from complete ruin during Prohibition, Congressional lawmakers had added a section to the Act that explicitly allowed householders to make "non-intoxicating [i.e., of no more than 0.5 percent alcohol by volume] . . . fruit juices for home consumption to the extent of 200 gallons [757.08 liters] annually."[7] Inspired by this odd provision, savvy vintners hit upon the idea of selling most of their harvests in the form of dehydrated grape "bricks" or raisin cakes. People could transform them into a refreshing juice just by adding water, but they could also turn them into a potent wine with relatively little effort.

To ensure that the buying public was aware of the wine-making potential of the bricks, grape producers sent demonstrators—usually attractive young women—to urban grocery stores all over the country. Ostensibly, their mission was to instruct customers how to turn the raisin cakes into juice and avoid illegal fermentation. If you do not wish your grape concentrate to become wine with a 12-percent-alcohol content, the demonstrators would solemnly admonish their listeners, after you dissolve the bricks in water, be sure *not* to pour the juice into a jug and close it in a dark cupboard for 60 days. Warning labels were also attached to each brick to caution consumers against inadvertently turning the rehydrated grapes into alcohol by allowing fermentation to occur.

Largely as a result of these not very subtle ploys to accentuate the wine-making possibilities of the raisin cakes, between 1925 and 1929, Americans chugged an estimated 678 million gallons (2,570 million liters) of home-fermented wine, "three times as much as all the domestic and imported wine they drank during the five years before prohibition," observes John Kobler.[8] America's newfound passion for homemade wine was excellent news for the nation's grape growers: In the country's premier grape-producing region, California's Napa Valley, growers expanded their acreage tenfold between 1920 and 1933, when national Prohibition ended. "The worst crime a child can commit," joked the popular American humorist, Will Rogers, "is to eat up the raisins that Dad brought home for fermenting purposes."[9]

NEAR BEER AND SOFT DRINKS: THE ALCOHOL INDUSTRY STRUGGLES TO COPE WITH PROHIBITION

Prohibition provided a welcome and unexpected boon to American grape growers. The Eighteenth Amendment and Volstead Act, however, had a profoundly negative economic impact on scores of other Americans with ties to the country's once-thriving alcoholic beverage industry. Tens of thousands of workers lost their jobs as breweries and distilleries across the nation closed their doors permanently. Untold numbers of bartenders, waiters, teamsters, and saloon owners also found themselves suddenly unemployed. In 1920, a letter to the editor of the New York *Daily News* blasted the seeming indifference of the Prohibitionists toward the plight of those whose livelihoods had been destroyed: "It is a wonder to me that the Prohibitionists can sleep," the anonymous writer complained, "They have thrown thousands of honest men out of work and caused great hardships. Many of the men in breweries had families to support. Now they are hunting jobs."[10]

Not all of the nation's brewery workers found themselves pounding the pavement in search of employment after January 16, 1920. Although the vast majority of the 1,300 breweries that had existed in America on the eve of Prohibition had gone under by the early 1920s, a few of the largest and best-known ones, including Anheuser-Busch, Miller, Schlitz, Pabst, and Coors did manage to remain afloat throughout the Volstead

Era. At first these businesses had focused on manufacturing near beer, the only beer that remained legal in the United States after the dry statutes went into effect.

To create near beer, which was supposed to have an alcohol content of 0.5 percent or less, breweries first made conventional beer, and then boiled off most of the alcohol. In the process of extracting the alcohol, brewers also boiled off the beer's esters, chemical compounds that give beer and other fermented drinks their distinctive flavor. As a result, near beer not only lacked the kick of regular beer, but it was also virtually tasteless. Not surprisingly, the low-alcohol beverage never caught on with the American public, and production of near beer declined steadily during the 1920s from a peak of 300,000 million gallons (1.1 billion liters) in 1921 to just 100,000 million gallons (3.79 million liters) in 1929.

As Anheuser-Busch and the other big breweries gradually turned away from the manufacture of near beer during the 1920s, they refit their operations to produce a variety of strictly nonalcoholic products. The most popular of these included yeast, malt syrup, candy, cheese, ice cream, and soft drinks such as ginger ale, root beer, and chocolate soda.

THE RISE OF THE SPEAKEASY

To the delight of the Anti-Saloon League and other drys, national Prohibition brought about the swift demise not only of the vast majority of America's distilleries and breweries but also its saloons. Yet even as federal agents were padlocking shut saloons across the nation during the winter of 1920, thousands of new underground drinking places that sold alcohol by the glass or bottle were springing up in America's cities and larger towns. Nicknamed blind pigs, gin joints, and most often, speakeasies, from the street these clandestine barrooms looked like private dwellings or businesses. One popular Detroit speakeasy was even disguised as a funeral parlor. When a customer tapped on the door of a speakeasy, a doorman would peer through the

During Prohibition, patrons sit at the bar of an unidentifed speakeasy while being served by a pair of bartenders in light-colored jackets in New York City in 1933. In contrast to the working class saloons of the pre-Prohibition era, speakeasies usually attracted a more prosperous clientele.

peephole to see if he recognized the knocker. If he did not, the customer would softly say a password or the name of a regular patron—hence the term *speakeasy*.

Unlike the saloons of pre-Prohibition days, speakeasies generally catered to a middle- or upper-class clientele. More often than not, the working men who had frequented the old neighborhood saloons could not afford to purchase the illegal liquor sold at speakeasies or pay the hefty cover charge many of them demanded from customers just to get inside. Often characterized as America's wettest city during Prohibition, New York City boasted some of the most expensive and fashionable speakeasies in the nation, including the famed 21 Club, which operated out of an elegant, four-story Manhattan townhouse. These upscale watering holes often served gourmet

One of New York City's most fashionable restaurants, the 21 Club, started out as a Prohibition Era speakeasy. Its founders were two youthful cousins from the city's West Side, Charlie Berns and Jack Kriendler. Under the skillful management of Berns and Kriendler, the elegant brownstone at 21 West Fifty-Second Street rapidly became one of the most popular and exclusive speakeasies in Manhattan, a place to see and be seen while patrons enjoyed the highest quality Canadian and European liquor.

Although Prohibition agents raided the 21 Club on a number of different occasions, Berns and Kriendler always managed to outsmart them. The cousins' elaborate security measures included multiple alarm buttons in the front lobby so, if raiders successfully prevented one of the alarms from being activated, the doorman could easily press another. Liquor stores were kept in five separate hiding places, which could only be accessed through concealed doors. The most famous of these liquor caches was the secret wine cellar. Located in the basement of the adjoining building, the 21's extensive wine cellar lay behind a cleverly concealed 5,000-pound (2,268-kilogram) door, which could only be opened by inserting a long metal rod into a miniscule hole in a certain brick. Years after Prohibition was repealed, Charlie Berns gave author John Kobler a tour of his establishment and reminisced about the speakeasy's complex and highly effective security system:

> We had this engineer we trusted, and he installed a series of contraptions for us that worked on different mechanical or

meals along with the illegal booze and featured live entertainment by well-known singers, dancers, and bands. Among their clientele were many of the nation's most glamorous celebrities,

electrical impulses. For example, the shelves behind the bar rested on tongue blocks. In case of a raid the bartender could press a button that released the blocks, letting the shelves fall backward and dropping the bottles down a chute. As they fell, they hit against angle irons projecting from the sides of the chute and smashed. At the bottom were rocks and a pile of sand through which the liquor seeped, leaving not a drop of evidence. In addition, when the button was pressed, an alarm bell went off, warning everybody to drink up fast. . . .

The most important [security device] was the secret door to our wine cellar. [At this point Berns took Kobler down to the basement, where, pausing before a brick wall, he pulled out a thin steel rod out of his pocket.] Unless you knew exactly where to look, all you can see are solid walls, no visible cracks of any kind. But there's this tiny aperture here. You'd have to have an eagle eye. [He put the rod into the opening.] When I push this a little further in, you'll hear a noise. That's the tongue lock being released on the other side. . . . This is the only entrance or exit. No other way in or out. If the mechanism broke, we'd have to dig through the concrete and pull out the whole lock. But that never happened. And no agent ever discovered the cache either. We still keep the contraption because people like to come down here and see the way things were in the old days.*

*Excerpted from John Kobler's interview with Charlie Berns in *Ardent Spirits,* p. 231.

including Broadway, vaudeville, and silent film stars, professional athletes, and even politicians such as New York City's mayor between 1926 and 1932, the fun-loving and defiantly wet Jimmy "Beau James" Walker.

WOMEN AND SPEAKEASIES

Respectable females had shunned the boisterous, predominantly working-class saloons of pre-Prohibition days. Yet middle- and upper-class women, particularly in bigger cities such as New York, flocked to the new speakeasies. Most of the speakeasy's female patrons were "flappers," as the independent-minded and unconventional young women of the fun-loving Roaring Twenties were popularly nicknamed. The taste for illegal alcohol and speakeasies was so strongly associated with the flapper, writes Michael Lerner, that speakeasies "became a motif as central to her popular depiction as bobbed hair, short skirts, and rolled stockings; . . . drinking became a new way for women . . . to express their 'smartness' and sophistication."[11]

Although most speakeasies—like the vast majority of American businesses at the time—were owned and managed by men, several of the country's best-known speakeasy hostesses were women. New York City's hard-drinking nightlife was presided over by three colorful females: Belle Livingston, a former showgirl whose spacious establishment included Ping-Pong tables and a miniature golf course; torch singer Helen Morgan, who fronted the trendy Chez Morgan; and last but not least, Mary Louise Cecilia "Texas" Guinan, who played mistress of ceremonies at several of the city's premier watering holes, including the Club El Fey, the Argonaut, and the Salon Royal.

A onetime silent-film actress and circus bronco rider, Texas Guinan was famous for her ebullient personality and sassy trademark greeting to her clubs' big spending clientele: "Hello, Sucker!" Guinan's nickname for her customers was apt. The Club El Fey and other speakeasies over which she presided charged exorbitant prices, including $2 for a pitcher of water

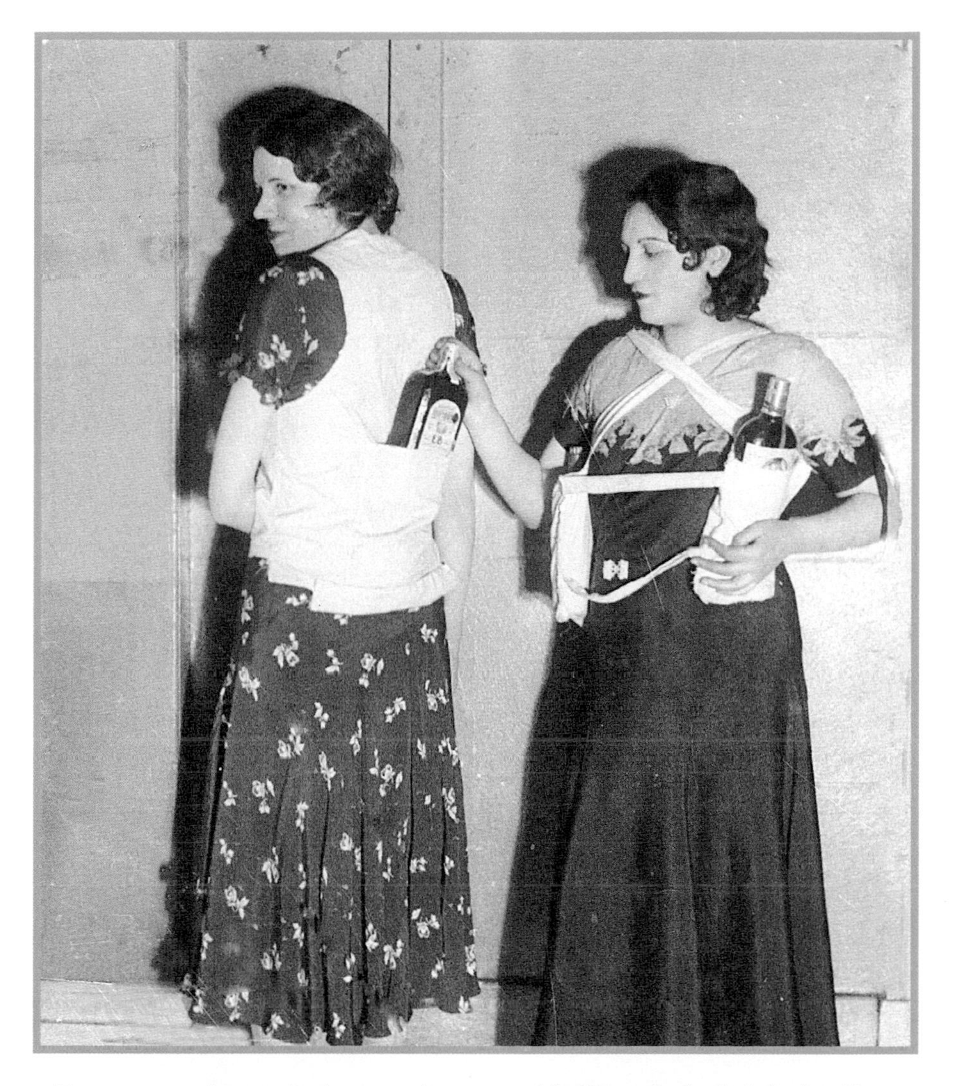

Two women demonstrate ways to conceal bottles of alcohol during Prohibition. Though respectable women had shunned the boisterous saloons of pre-Prohibition days, middle- and upper-class women, particularly in bigger cities, flocked to speakeasies during Prohibition.

and $25 for a quart (.95 liters) of "champagne," actually carbonated cider spiked with alcohol. (In today's dollars, the water and the phony champagne would cost about $24 and $300, respectively.) At the height of her popularity as a speakeasy hostess in the mid-twenties, Texas reportedly earned $7,000 a week: "Where the hell would I be without prohibition?" she was fond of saying.[12]

Texas Guinan was not the only American who made a great deal of money from Prohibition, by any means. The bootleggers—manufacturers, transporters, and sellers of illegal liquor—who supplied Club El Fey and the nation's tens of thousands of other speakeasies also became rich from the unpopular dry laws. Indeed, some of them, like lawyer-turned-bootlegger George Remus and Al Capone, arguably the most famous gangster in history, would become millionaires many times over before the Prohibition Era came to an end.

Bootleggers, Rumrunners, and Gangsters

The refusal of millions of American men and women, particularly in the nation's cities, to comply with Prohibition created a large and highly lucrative market for bootleggers. Although it was risky work, bootlegging could also be extraordinarily profitable; alcoholic beverages sold for anywhere from 2 to 10 times more after January 16, 1920, than they had before the United States went dry. Bootleggers usually obtained their illegal liquor in one of three ways: They smuggled it in from other countries; they distilled it themselves or paid others to distill it for them; or they pilfered legally manufactured liquor, such as medicinal whiskey. One of the most colorful and successful bootleggers of the early Prohibition Era, George Remus, made tens of millions of dollars by choosing the last of these three options.

GEORGE REMUS CASHES IN ON MEDICINAL LIQUOR

During the 1920s, many Americans, including numerous physicians, still believed in the medicinal benefits of alcohol, and particularly of whiskey. People thought that liquor, when taken in moderate amounts, soothed frazzled nerves, aided digestion, and shortened the duration of head colds. Reflecting the popular faith in liquor's therapeutic value, the Volstead Act allowed physicians to prescribe spirits to their patients at a rate of one pint (.47 liter) per person every 10 days.

From the beginning, unscrupulous patients, physicians, and pharmacists found ways to exploit this loophole in the Prohibition laws by requesting, writing, and filling mountains of phony prescriptions. Most of this deceptively obtained liquor was then sold to bootleggers or a private clientele. In 1929 alone, U.S. pharmacists filled a whopping 11 million medical prescriptions for hard liquor. Yet the vast majority of men and women who dealt in bogus liquor prescriptions during Prohibition were small-time operators. Ambitious and well-funded bootleggers who sought to make large sums of money from the medicinal liquor loophole did not bother with the fake prescription racket. Instead, they purchased entire distilleries and their inventories, and no bootlegger bought out more distilleries or made more money from them than George Remus.

The son of German immigrants, George Remus grew up in a modest working-class neighborhood of Chicago. A diligent student of above-average ability, he trained as a pharmacist as a young man before he switched to law. By the start of Prohibition, Remus had become one of Chicago's most successful criminal defense attorneys, reportedly earning $50,000 (almost $600,000 in today's dollars) a year, but he wanted more. Several of his clients were bootleggers and, as Remus would later recall, "I was deeply impressed by the rapidity with which those men . . . piled up fortunes in the liquor business."[1]

Lured by the promise of quick money, Remus moved to Cincinnati in 1920 to try his hand at bootlegging. He had done his research and knew that the greater Cincinnati area contained a large percentage of those distilleries that had been licensed by the government to distribute medicinal whiskey. Using his life savings, Remus bought out one distillery after another with the intention of surreptitiously diverting their vast inventories to the underground liquor trade. By liberally bribing warehouse guards, Prohibition agents, and local policemen, Remus managed to sneak millions of gallons (liters) of whiskey ostensibly meant for medical uses out of his distilleries and sell the booze for much higher prices to speakeasies and other illegal retailers.

According to Edward Behr, Remus's bootlegging scheme was so lucrative that "within a few months of Prohibition, he was depositing tens of thousands of dollars a day into various bank accounts both in his own name and under aliases."[2] Remus and his second wife, Imogene, bought a 10-acre (4.05-hectare) estate in the city's most exclusive suburb and installed racing stables, a greenhouse, and an Olympic-size indoor pool of Italian marble, among other amenities. Determined to use their new wealth to gain entry into Cincinnati high society, the couple began to host decadently extravagant parties at their castle-like mansion, the "Marble Palace." The huge soirees inevitably featured lavish party favors for the guests, such as crisp $100 bills; diamond cufflinks; on one occasion, brand-new Pontiac automobiles; and plenty of illegal, high-quality liquor, even though Remus himself never drank.

By 1924, Remus owned a total of 14 distilleries in 5 states, including the celebrated Jack Daniels distillery in St. Louis, Missouri, and was said to be worth more than $50 million. Remus's luck ran out that year: A federal agent infiltrated his bootlegging empire, and the onetime criminal defense attorney was sentenced to three years in prison. To make matters worse, while Remus was incarcerated, Imogene Remus fell in love with the very same Prohibition agent who had nabbed her husband. She filed for a divorce, but before she moved out of the couple's

By the start of Prohibition, George Remus was one of Chicago's most successful criminal defense attorneys. Several of his clients were bootleggers; impressed with the fortunes they amassed, Remus decided to try his hand at bootlegging. Here, Remus is shown arriving at home after two years in the Atlanta Federal Penitentiary.

opulent Cincinnati home, she stripped the Marble Palace of all its expensive furniture and artwork and withdrew millions of dollars from her estranged husband's various bank accounts.

From his jail cell, Remus vowed revenge. On October 6, 1927, three days after his release from prison, he shot his estranged wife dead as she was heading to Domestic Relations Court for a divorce hearing. At the highly publicized murder trial that followed, Remus acted as his own attorney and more than proved his exceptional abilities as a criminal defense lawyer by convincing the jury to find him innocent by reason of temporary insanity. After he spent only six months in an Ohio state hospital for the criminally insane, Remus was declared miraculously cured and released. By this time, however, his bootlegging cronies had scattered and most of his fortune was gone. Shortly before Prohibition was repealed in 1933, the onetime bootlegging kingpin left Cincinnati for Kentucky, where he lived in relative obscurity until his death two decades later.

SMUGGLING IN LIQUOR FROM CANADA

Many more Prohibition Era bootleggers obtained their alcohol by smuggling the booze in from abroad—or paying others to sneak it in for them—than by buying up legal stocks of domestic liquor as George Remus did. The source of most of this contraband liquor was the United States' neighbor to the north. Indeed, Prohibition officials estimated that three-quarters of the alcohol smuggled into the country came from Canada, a major producer of beverage alcohol, and particularly whiskey, during the 1920s and early 1930s. In 1922 alone, the Prohibition Unit calculated, 1.5 million gallons (5.8 million liters) of bootleg Canadian whiskey made its way into the United States. Although a great deal of the contraband traveled overland by truck, automobile, train, or even horse-drawn wagon into the United States, the vast majority of Canadian liquor was ferried across the lakes and rivers that separate Michigan from the province of Ontario.

The most popular smuggling route between Michigan and Ontario was over the Detroit River, which separates the United States and Canadian cities of Detroit and Windsor. Less than a mile wide in some places, the Detroit River was a bootlegger's delight with scores of secluded coves and other inviting shelters and hiding places along its 28-mile- (45.06-kilometer-) long shore. During the early years of Prohibition, most smugglers along the Detroit River were small-time operators who transported their contraband in rowboats, skiffs, canoes, and homemade rafts. By the mid 1920s, however, criminal gangs had come to dominate the illegal river traffic between Windsor and the Motor City, using expensive high-powered motorboats to outrun the police boats and Internal Revenue cutters that lurked on the opposite shore.

The most powerful and ruthless of the various criminal groups that operated on the Detroit River during Prohibition was Detroit's notorious Purple Gang—young Russian immigrants, chiefly Jewish, who started out as pickpockets and shakedown artists before they graduated to bootlegging, armed robbery, and murder. During the early 1920s, the Purples built up a large fleet of speedboats for running Canadian booze to the Motor City. Yet the young gangsters seem to have devoted at least as much time and energy to hijacking other smugglers' cargoes as they did to transporting their own contraband.

"Hijacking was a jackpot" for the Purples, according to author Paul Kavieff, and any independent smuggler on the Detroit River risked being robbed at gunpoint by the heavily armed gang members who regularly patrolled the waterway.[3] The Purples were able to double their profits on every bottle that they stole or smuggled in by perfecting the Prohibition Era art of "cutting": diluting commercially produced alcoholic beverages with equal amounts of water, then adding food coloring and flavoring to restore the watered-down brew to something that at least vaguely resembled the real thing.

RUM ROW AND CAPTAIN BILL MCCOY

Although most of the foreign liquor that reached the United States after the Volstead Act went into effect came from Canada by way of the rivers and lakes that separate Ontario and Michigan, countless gallons of alcohol were also smuggled into the country over the open seas. Much of it came from French- and English-owned islands in the Atlantic and Caribbean, especially the tiny French archipelago of Saint-Pierre and Miquelon off the coast of Newfoundland, Canada, and the British territories of Jamaica and the Bahamas. Although they were just as likely to be smuggling whiskey or gin as rum, the captains and crews of the schooners, freighters, and other large vessels that transported the contraband were popularly known as rumrunners. Fearful of calling attention to their disreputable activities, rumrunners rarely attempted to dock and unload their illegal cargoes onshore. Instead, they would drop anchor several miles offshore just beyond U.S. territorial limits and wait for smaller, ship-to-shore boats to pick up the booze, usually under cover of night.

During the Prohibition Era, the international waters where the rumrunners waited for their bootlegger customers were nicknamed rum rows. The busiest rum rows were located off the northeastern coast of the United States near New Jersey and Long Island, undoubtedly because of their proximity to New York City and its numerous speakeasies. Nonetheless, rum rows existed outside almost every major metropolis on both the Pacific and the Atlantic coasts, with the cities of the Pacific shoreline primarily serviced by rumrunners from Mexico to the south and Vancouver, Canada to the north. "People would stand on a spit of land, perhaps with binoculars," writes Eric Burns, "and peer out at their local Rum Row as they would any other tourist attraction."[4]

Alcohol was smuggled into the United States in a variety of ways, including within the tanker shown here, docked in Hoboken, New Jersey. When this ship was caught, federal agents oversaw the removal of the illicit whiskey, which was pumped out of the boat and into the Hudson River.

Captain William "Bill" McCoy was the most famous rum-runner of the Prohibition Era and, by his own account, the inventor of the rum row system. Before the Eighteenth Amendment, McCoy, a sailing enthusiast and former member of the merchant marine, made his living building yachts for wealthy clients in Jacksonville, Florida. When Prohibition came along, McCoy saw an outstanding opportunity to make a lot of money in a short period of time, like his fellow teetotaler, George

Remus. By 1921, he was making regular voyages from Florida to the Bahamas in the South and St. Pierre and Miquelon in the North to pick up cargoes of liquor, which he then transported to various rum rows up and down the eastern seaboard. Because he only dealt in the highest-quality whiskey, McCoy quickly became one of the most sought-after offshore liquor suppliers on the East Coast. Indeed, the expression "the real McCoy," may have first been coined to describe Bill McCoy's invariably top-notch liquor, which stood in sharp contrast to the water-downed brew that many rumrunners tried to pawn off on their customers.

McCoy made hundreds of thousands of dollars from his rum-running ventures during the early 1920s, but in 1924, his lucrative smuggling career came to an abrupt end when federal authorities finally caught up with him. After he served nine months in jail, McCoy returned home to Florida and announced that he was giving up rum-running for good. "This is not repentance," he insisted. "If the racket today promised half the fun I've had out of it in the past, I'd jump into it tomorrow. But the game has altered. . . . Modern efficiency does away with individual enterprise and the spirit of adventure. Big business wants safety and results, and present-day rum-running is big business."[5]

When McCoy talked about the takeover of rumrunning by "big business," according to John Kobler, he really meant organized crime. What had long "set McCoy apart from the majority of his fellow contrabandists was his freedom from the control of gangsters," said Kobler: "He prided himself on never paying a cent for protection to any racketeer."[6] By the mid-twenties, however, McCoy's favorite rum row, the waters from Atlantic City north to New York harbor, had fallen largely under the sway of New York gang bosses like William "Big Bill" Dwyer. Unlike McCoy, Dwyer and his fellow mobsters had the financial means to purchase and maintain extensive fleets of oceangoing ships to gather liquor from foreign ports, as well as top-of-the-line speedboats capable of consistently outrunning Coast Guard patrols on their way to shore.

As the 1920s wore on, fewer and fewer independent smugglers proved able to compete with the well-organized and funded criminal outfits, especially because a substantial cut of their profits typically ended up in the mobsters' pockets as "protection fees." Supposedly, these payments bought the independent smugglers protection from pirates by the mobsters' gun-toting thugs, but in reality, they just guaranteed that the thugs would not hijack the rumrunners' cargoes themselves.

BOOTLEGGERS AND THE ILLEGAL MANUFACTURE OF ALCOHOL

During the Prohibition Era, many ordinary Americans concocted their own hooch, beer, or wine. Bootleggers also frequently made the liquor that they sold, or hired others to produce it for them, but typically on a much larger and more sophisticated scale than the do-it-yourselfers with their washtub stills and dehydrated grape bricks. Most bootleggers focused on distilling liquor not only because spirits were typically simpler and quicker to produce than beer or wine, but also because they contained significantly more alcohol by volume. That meant that hard liquor was not only less expensive to transport but also easier to hide.

Bootleggers set up their clandestine stills in every spot imaginable: grain silos, unused warehouses, even the hollowed-out trunk of a giant redwood tree in the northern California wilderness. Some of the stills were capable of turning out 50 gallons (189.27 liters) to 100 gallons (378.54 liters) of liquor per day, and as America's long dry spell dragged on, the amount of illegal distilling increased steadily. In 1921, Prohibition agents seized approximately 96,000 stills from bootleggers; by 1930, government seizures topped 280,000. Nonetheless, Prohibition Administrator Lincoln Andrew believed that his agents were probably only ferreting out one of every ten of the illegal devices.

Some bootleg liquor was produced from stolen industrial alcohol, which was manufactured in numerous plants throughout the United States during the Prohibition Era. By law, industrial alcohol had to be denatured—made unfit for human consumption—usually by adding poisonous chemicals such as benzene or methanol. Bootleggers either washed or redistilled the pilfered industrial alcohol to take out the harmful substances and make it drinkable, or they hired chemists to carry out the purification process for them. Unfortunately, improperly washed industrial alcohol was all too common during Prohibition; it is believed to have blinded or killed thousands of unsuspecting drinkers. According to one report, more than 700 New Yorkers died in 1926 alone as a result of ingesting poisoned alcohol.

Although most bootleggers focused on hard liquor, some bought out failing breweries, where they covertly produced illegal full-strength beer. Others collaborated with established brewers who were ostensibly producing only near beer but were in fact also surreptitiously turning out just as much regular beer. Needling beer—restoring near beer to its original potency by spiking the barrels with distilled alcohol—was also a common practice among bootleggers.

PROHIBITION AND ORGANIZED CRIME

As the 1920s unfolded, more and more of the lucrative liquor smuggling and bootlegging trade fell under the control of organized crime rings. This trend was apparent by the middle of the decade in the violence that ensued when the Purple Gang took over the Detroit River smuggling route, and Dwyer and other Big Apple mobsters took over the New York area Rum Row. Long before the Eighteenth Amendment and the Volstead Act, gangsters had been running houses of prostitution and gambling joints, as well as dabbling in the narcotics trade in many of America's larger urban areas. Yet spurred on by the staggering profits to be made in black-market liquor, the scale

(continues on page 78)

AL CAPONE
(1899–1947)

Leader in Organized Crime

Arguably the best-known gangster of all time, Al Capone was born Alphonse Capone, in Brooklyn, New York, on January 17, 1899, the fourth of nine children of poor Italian immigrant parents. After he dropped out of school at age 14, Al joined Manhattan's notorious Five Points Gang and befriended the gang lieutenant, Frankie Yale. Yale soon became Al's mentor, hiring the burly teenager to work as a bouncer at his seedy Coney Island saloon. One night, a knife-wielding customer assaulted Capone in a dispute over a woman. The attack left the 18-year-old with three long, ugly scars on the left side of his face and accounted for his later nickname: Scarface.

In 1919, Johnny Torrio, a business associate of Yale's, invited Capone to work for him in Chicago. Torrio had moved to the Windy City from New York several years earlier to help his uncle by marriage, mob czar Big Jim Colosimo, run his thriving prostitution ring. Capone's business acumen and ruthlessness so impressed Torrio that he soon made the young gangster his right-hand man. Within a year of Capone's arrival in Chicago, Colosimo was gunned down, almost certainly at Torrio's behest, leaving Torrio and his new lieutenant in charge of Colosimo criminal syndicate. Torrio and Capone immediately focused their attention on bootlegging, which Colosimo had been reluctant to take up despite the huge profits it promised.

After he was almost killed by rival mobsters, Torrio decided to retire in 1925, turning over his lucrative bootlegging, gambling, prostitution, and protection rackets to Capone. Capone rapidly expanded Torrio's underworld network until he controlled hundreds of speakeasies, distilleries, breweries, racetracks, and brothels throughout the greater Chicago area. To protect his expanding empire, said Mark Lender and James Martin, "Capone had perhaps a thousand men working directly for him (some of whom he kept busy fighting off or eliminating rival gangs), as well as numerous city police and other officials on his unofficial payroll."* Touted as "Public Enemy Number One" in the press, Capone's brutal methods and spectacular wealth, along with the apparent inability of local law enforcement authorities to stop him, soon made the mob kingpin a national celebrity. "I make my money by supplying a public demand," an unrepentant Capone declared: "If I break the law, my customers, who number hundreds of the best people in Chicago, are as guilty as I am. The only difference between us is that I sell and they buy. Everybody calls me a racketeer. I call myself a businessman. When I sell liquor, it's bootlegging. When my patrons serve it on a silver tray on Lake Shore Drive, it's hospitality.**

At the beginning of 1929, Al Capone was at the height of his influence, but the infamous Saint Valentine's Day Massacre on February 14 of that year signaled the beginning of the end of his extraordinary rags-to-riches saga. Americans were horrified by the brazenness and brutality of the execution-style killings in which five of Capone's henchmen, some disguised as police officers, lined up seven members of rival mobster Bugs Moran's gang against a garage wall and riddled them with machine-gun fire. Police could not pin the massacre on Capone, but just about everyone, including Moran himself, believed he masterminded the killings. Under enormous pressure to do something about the escalating gang violence in Chicago, President Herbert Hoover ordered the Treasury Department to investigate Capone's financial dealings.

In 1931, Capone was convicted of income tax evasion and sentenced to 11 years in prison. He served most of his sentence in Alcatraz, California's allegedly escape-proof federal penitentiary.

(continues)

(continued)

Capone was released from Alcatraz in 1939 because of his deteriorating mental health, which was the result of untreated syphilis that had invaded his nervous system. He spent the rest of his life in virtual seclusion in his home on Palm Island, Florida, finally dying of heart failure on January 25, 1947, at the age of 48.

---

*Lender and Martin, *Drinking in America,* p. 141.
**Quoted in Allen, *Only Yesterday,* p. 214.

(continued from page 75)
and scope of organized crime grew at an unprecedented and alarming rate after 1920.

Virtually every major U.S. city, at least in the more populous eastern half of the nation, had its criminal gangs and mob kingpins during the Prohibition Era. From Boston to Kansas City, St. Paul to Miami, gangsters controlled tens of thousands of illegal speakeasies, distilleries, breweries, and "cutting plants," where smuggled liquor was diluted to maximize profits. They also controlled vast fleets of boats and trucks for transporting bootleg alcohol into and around the country. New York City was home to dozens of gangs with ties to the illegal liquor trade and some of the most influential and famous mob bosses in the nation, including Charlie "Lucky" Luciano, Meyer Lansky, and Benjamin "Bugsy" Siegel. Even so, no Prohibition Era city was more closely associated in the public mind with organized crime—and the bloody gang warfare that all too often accompanied it—than Chicago.

At the beginning of Prohibition, the powerful South Side mobster, Johnny Torrio, had hammered out agreements with

Al Capone (left) looks at the camera as he walks out of Federal Court in Chicago with his attorney Michael Ahern on October 11, 1931. Although he was never successfully prosecuted for the racketeering that was the cause of his notoriety, Capone was convicted of tax evasion in 1931.

Chicago's other crime bosses, providing each group with a share of the city's illegal liquor market. Soon, profit-hungry mobsters began to encroach on one another's territory, and violence among rival gangs skyrocketed. By 1925, the most ruthless and powerful of Chicago's entire mob was a 26-year-old Brooklyn native named Al Capone. The man whom Chicago newspapers would dub "Public Enemy Number One" was reaping an estimated $60 million in profits annually; he dominated the city's bootlegging business, as well as most of its other rackets, including gambling, loan sharking, and prostitution, by the end of the decade. Allegedly, Capone was able to consolidate his power by engineering the assassinations of dozens of his underworld competitors, including seven members of George "Bugs" Moran's gang, who were gunned down on February 14, 1929, in the infamous "Saint Valentine's Day Massacre."

The brutal and highly publicized Valentine's Day shootings shocked and disgusted not only Chicago but the entire nation. Many people placed the blame for the terrifying increase in mob violence during the twenties squarely on Prohibition and the underground liquor trade that it gave rise to. Public disenchantment with the Eighteenth Amendment was nothing new in February 1929; over the past several years, increasing numbers of Americans had been openly questioning the wisdom of national Prohibition. For the first time since the Volstead Act went into effect in January 1920, it appeared to many wets that the end of Prohibition might actually be in sight.

The Road to Repeal

By 1929, a decade after ratification of the Eighteenth Amendment, Prohibition's enemies were not only more numerous, but also better organized and funded than ever before. Much of the credit for this belongs to business tycoon Pierre du Pont, who was the head of the country's largest anti-Prohibition organization, the Association Against the Prohibition Amendment (AAPA). Although he had once generously supported the Anti-Saloon League, du Pont claimed that his change of heart about Prohibition was rooted in concerns over growing governmental intrusion into people's personal lives. Yet economic self-interest also clearly played a vital role in the millionaire industrialist's newfound commitment to repeal the Eighteenth Amendment from the mid 1920s on. During the first half of the decade, federal income taxes rose sharply, and du Pont's enormous wealth placed him well within the highest tax bracket. Legalizing the manufacture and sale of alcoholic beverages and then taxing them heavily would give the federal government a major new source of funding and "permit the total abolition of income tax, both personal and corporate," du Pont reasoned.[1]

TURNING PUBLIC OPINION AGAINST PROHIBITION: THE AAPA AND THE MEDIA

Founded in 1918 by retired naval officer William Strayon, the AAPA focused during its first eight years on denouncing the Eighteenth Amendment as unconstitutional. It argued that the central government extended its power at the expense of local control, an ideologically based approach that lacked popular appeal. When du Pont assumed control of the AAPA in 1926, he brought his own money to the association's anti-Prohibition campaign, as well as that of the other wealthy corporate leaders and heavy taxpayers he persuaded to join the organization. He also brought new public relations savvy. Under du Pont's shrewd direction, notes historian John Burnham, the AAPA became remarkably adept at working the mass media:

> Much effort went into attitude and image in the manner of slick national advertising (as opposed to rational persuasion). By setting up sources for newspaper reporters, for example, and by making the copy moderate and plausible (although not necessarily accurate), the officials of the AAPA were able to manipulate the press in a remarkable way. . . . Innocent-appearing stories, such as those suggesting that alcohol could benefit humanity by serving as automobile fuel along with gasoline, had their origin with AAPA publicists who saw that any material that would generate favorable associations in connection with alcohol would benefit the repeal cause (and in the case of alcohol for gasoline, appeal in the farm belt that was strongly dry). And of course the publicists kept up

> a high volume of releases that in one way or another called attention to violation of the law or suggested that Prohibition was a failure or had undesirable side effects.[2]

By the late 1920s, the American press, although previously supportive of the dry cause, now turned overwhelmingly against the Eighteenth Amendment to the enormous satisfaction of du Pont and the AAPA, not to mention the struggling brewing and distilling industries. Stories that cast Prohibition in a favorable light became increasingly rare, particularly in urban-based newspapers. At the same time, the press thoroughly covered every negative side effect of America's dry experiment: the perils of ingesting tainted moonshine, corruption among federal agents, and increased drinking among college students enticed by the thrill of buying bootleg liquor. "Headlines such as 'Dry Agent Accused,' 'Prohibition Graft,' 'Enforcement Farce,' 'Drunken Children,' and even 'Prohibition Failure' appeared consistently in metropolitan newspapers," according to Burnham. "Prohibition was big news only when it was being defied," he concludes, "not when it was working."[3] Articles about gruesome gangland killings and innocent bystanders caught in the crossfire between bootleggers and overzealous lawmen were especially common. Although these sensational and often exaggerated accounts of Prohibition-related violence were obviously designed to sell papers, they convinced many Americans that, instead of diminishing crime, as dry activists had always claimed Prohibition would do, the Volstead Act actually seemed to be boosting it.

During the late 1920s and early 1930s, motion pictures and the written media encouraged the general perception that Prohibition was failing by "implying that plenty of drinking was taking place, especially within the upper classes of society," observes David Kyvic.[4] A survey taken in 1930 revealed that drinking played a role in 80 percent of the movies released during the previous year. "We took the position that motion pictures should depict and reflect American life, and cocktail parties and speakeasies were definitely a part of that life," declared MGM director Clarence Brown in 1933: "I believe that it was the motion picture, showing that in spite of prohibition, liquor was an immense factor in American life, that had a great deal to do with changing sentiment on the question."[5]

THE HERCULEAN TASK OF ENFORCING PROHIBITION

Scholars agree that the media's portrayal of Prohibition as a nearly unmitigated flop helped shift public opinion toward repeal of the Eighteenth Amendment during the last half of the 1920s. By the late 1920s, it was not difficult to convince most Americans to accept the idea that Prohibition was failing for the simple reason that the Volstead Act had proven virtually impossible to enforce.

From the outset of Prohibition, it was clear that compliance with the new liquor laws was going to be extremely difficult. Indeed, the task that faced the Prohibition Bureau was almost unimaginable. Agents were expected to patrol more than 18,000 miles (28,968 kilometers) of inland borders and coastline with only minimal assistance from the U.S. Coast Guard and Customs Service; hunt down hundreds of thousands of underground stills, breweries, and speakeasies; and scrutinize every business that used industrial alcohol and every physician who prescribed medicinal whiskey to ensure that legally manufactured liquor was not being diverted to illegal purposes. For the Prohibition Bureau to have any hope of effectively enforcing the Volstead Act, maintained its first commissioner, John Kramer, Congress would have to earmark enough funds to support a small army of field agents. Instead, reflecting the cost-cutting fiscal policies of the era, Congress allocated between $6 and $12 million annually to the Prohibition Bureau during the 1920s, enough to support only about 1,500 to 3,000 agents at discouragingly small yearly salaries.

State financial support for Prohibition enforcement was also woefully inadequate. Almost all of the states passed "baby Volstead" laws during the early 1920s to bolster the national Prohibition statutes. Penny-pinching state legislators, however, were even more reluctant to spend money on enforcing dry laws than Congress. Indeed, as Prohibition dragged on and it became increasingly evident that only a small percentage of smugglers and other violators were being caught, many state legislators balked at committing any money at all to local enforcement. As early as 1923, New York repealed its baby Volstead laws in frustration and handed over all responsibility for enforcing Prohibition within the state to the federal government. Over the next six years, several other states, including Wisconsin, Montana, and Massachusetts, would follow New York's lead and revoke their baby Volstead laws, as well.

Inadequate governmental funding for enforcement was directly linked to what was probably Prohibition's most serious public relations problem: widespread corruption among Prohibition Bureau employees. Not all Prohibition agents were on the take by any means; in fact, two New York City agents, Izzy Einstein and Moe Smith, became national celebrities for their unswerving dedication and honesty, as well as their inventive use of disguise to infiltrate bootlegging operations. Nevertheless, the low salaries at the Prohibition Bureau tempted hundreds of federal agents to supplement their meager incomes with bribes from bootleggers, speakeasy owners, and other Volstead violators hoping to escape prosecution. "During the first six years of Prohibition," observes Thomas Pegram, "one of every twelve Bureau agents was fired for taking bribes . . . or other corrupt acts."[6] Mabel Walker Willebrandt, the assistant attorney general in charge of Prohibition enforcement from 1920 until her resignation in 1929, was dismayed by the low moral standards of Bureau employees. Far too many agents, she complained, "are as devoid of honesty and integrity as the bootlegging fraternity . . . [and] no more to be trusted with a

Police officers Isadore "Izzy" Einstein, left, and Moe Smith, who worked together as prohibition agents from 1920 to 1925, are shown on March 31, 1931. The two made 4,392 arrests, of which 95 percent ended in convictions, in their career during the Prohibition Era.

commission to enforce the laws of the United States and to carry a gun than the notorious bandit Jesse James."[7]

WOMEN AND THE REPEAL MOVEMENT

During the spring of 1929, the repeal movement gained an important new ally: wealthy New York socialite and president of the Women's National Republican Club, Pauline Sabin. Blasting the Eighteenth Amendment for promoting "crime, . . . hypocrisy, and corruption," in May 1929, Sabin announced her intention to form a new repeal organization composed exclusively of females, the Women's Organization for National

Prohibition Reform (WONPR).[8] In common with Sabin, most of the WONPR's leaders, like the head of the Delaware chapter, Mrs. Pierre du Pont, came from upper-class backgrounds. The organization's rank-and-file membership, however, included women from all social and economic groups and almost every part of the country. By the early 1930s, WONPR chapters existed in 43 states and the District of Columbia.

The widespread popularity of the WONPR and the repeal cause generally among women shocked and dismayed the Prohibitionists. When ratification of the Nineteenth Amendment in August 1920 finally brought American women the vote, in light of past female support for temperance, the Anti-Saloon League and other anti-liquor groups assumed that female voters would overwhelmingly back the dry cause. Drys, however, had not reckoned on the enormous cultural and social changes that would take place in the United States during the rebellious decade following approval of the Nineteenth Amendment. During the Roaring Twenties, many American women scorned traditional ideas about proper female behavior and roles, including the long-held beliefs that women should act as society's moral guardians and that respectable females never drank in public.

As more and more American women jumped on the repeal bandwagon during the late 1920s and early 1930s, alarmed drys became increasingly harsh in their criticism of Sabin and other females who demanded an end to Prohibition. *The American Independent*, a dry periodical from Kentucky, went so far as to claim that "you cannot find two dozen women in the State who openly advocate the Repeal of the Eighteenth Amendment, who is not either a drunkard, or whose home life is not immoral, or who does not expect to get in the liquor business when and if it is again legalized."[9]

Despite dry attempts to discredit female Prohibition opponents, by 1931 the WONPR boasted a membership of more than one million, making it the single largest repeal organization in the country. Heartened by the WONPR's success, other repeal groups, ranging from the big–business-dominated AAPA to working class organizations sponsored by various labor unions, stepped up their own anti-Prohibition campaigns. Two different developments greatly aided their efforts: first, the severe economic downturn known as the Great Depression, and second, an embarrassing scandal that involved the leader of the nation's premier dry organization, the Anti-Saloon League.

THE GREAT DEPRESSION AND A DRY SCANDAL

In October 1929, the unprecedented economic prosperity that had characterized the Roaring Twenties ended abruptly with the disastrous collapse of stock-market prices on the New York Stock Exchange. In the aftermath of the stock market crash, tens of thousands of banks and businesses failed and unemployment rates soared, plunging the United States into the worst economic crisis in its history and casting the repeal issue in a whole new light. Quick to see an opportunity, repeal supporters asserted that the millions of dollars devoted to enforcing the Volstead Act each year would be far better used to aid the nation's growing numbers of hungry and homeless. Moreover, they pointed out, legalizing the manufacture and sale of liquor would put scores of unemployed Americans back to work, and new federal and state liquor taxes would generate much needed additional revenue for fiscally challenged governments. Millions of Americans apparently found these arguments compelling because, by April 1932, a public opinion poll conducted by *Literary Digest* magazine indicated that most of the nation had turned against Prohibition. Almost 75 percent of the more than 4.6 million votes cast in the *Digest* poll supported repeal of the Eighteenth Amendment.

The declining fortunes of the single largest anti-liquor group in the nation, the Anti-Saloon League, further strengthened the repeal movement after 1929. Following the death of

(continues on page 92)

In 1928, Herbert Hoover was elected president of the United States. Although Hoover was committed to Prohibition, during his campaign, he promised to form a special panel to investigate and make recommendations about what he described as America's "great social and economic experiment, noble in motive and far reaching in purpose."

After almost two years of investigation, on January 19, 1931, the Wickersham Commission finally offered its report on Prohibition. Although the five-volume report detailed the widespread corruption within the Prohibition Bureau, the growing public disdain for the Volstead Act, and the immense difficulties in halting the bootleggers' increasingly sophisticated and profitable operations, the Commission hesitated to recommend repeal of the Eighteenth Amendment or even significant modification of the Volstead Act.

Shortly after the Commission released its findings, popular American humorist Franklin P. Adams aptly summarized wet disdain for the report in a poem published in the New York *World.* Entitled "The Wickersham Report," Adams's poem mocked the panel's plainly contradictory conclusions:

> Prohibition is an awful flop.
> We like it.
> It can't stop what it's meant to stop.
> We like it.
> It's left a trail of graft and slime,
> It don't prohibit worth a dime,
> It's filled our land with vice and crime,
> Nevertheless, we're for it.*

The following excerpts from the 1931 *Report on the Enforcement of the Prohibition Laws of the United States National Commission on Law Observance and Enforcement,* summarize some of the key weaknesses that the Wickersham Commission identified in Prohibition enforcement during its 18-month-long investigation:

BAD FEATURES OF THE PRESENT SITUATION . . .

CORRUPTION

As to corruption it is sufficient to refer to the reported decisions of the courts during the past decade in all parts of the country, which reveal a succession of prosecutions for conspiracies, sometimes involving the police, prosecuting and administrative organizations of whole communities; to the flagrant corruption disclosed in connection with diversions of industrial alcohol and unlawful production of beer; . . . to the revelations as to police corruption in every type of municipality, large and small, throughout the decade. . . .

ECONOMIC DIFFICULTIES

Another type of difficulties [is] economic. . . . The constant cheapening and simplification of production of alcohol and of alcoholic drinks, the improvement in quality of what may be made by illicit means the diffusion of knowledge as to how to produce liquor and the perfection of organization of unlawful manufacture and distribution have developed faster than the means of enforcement. But of even more significance is the margin of profit in smuggling liquor, in diversion of industrial alcohol, in illicit distilling and brewing, in bootlegging, and in the manufacture and sale of products of which the bulk goes into illicit . . . making of liquor. This profit makes possible systematic and organized violation of the National Prohibition Act on a large scale and offers rewards on a par with the most important legitimate industries. . . .

PSYCHOLOGICAL DIFFICULTIES

A number of causes of resentment . . . at the law or at features of its enforcement raise difficulties for national prohibition. A

(continues)

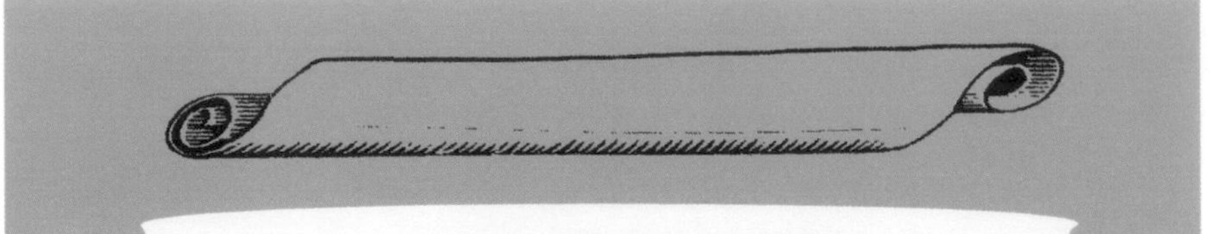

considerable part of the public [was] irritated at a constitutional "don't" in a matter where they saw no moral question. . . . In consequence many of the best citizens in every community, on whom we rely habitually for the upholding of law and order, are at most lukewarm as to the National Prohibition Act. Many who are normally law-abiding are led to an attitude hostile to the statute by a feeling that repression and interference with private conduct area carried too far. This is aggravated in many of the larger cities by a feeling that other parts of the land are seeking to impose ideas of conduct upon them and to mold city life to what are considered to be their provincial conceptions. . . .

---

*Quoted in Lerner, *Dry Manhattan,* p. 274.

(continued from page 88)
Wayne Wheeler, the League's influential leader, in 1927, the organization fell under the sway of Bishop James Cannon of the Methodist Episcopal Church. Narrow-minded and pompous, "Bishop Cannon was a difficult man to like," observes Edward Behr. "This puritanical Protestant Ayatollah disapproved of most if not all pleasurable activities. . . . He was against dancing, theatricals, and any games, sports, or art that provided glimpses of 'the female person.'"[10] Cannon also spoke out strongly against the Roman Catholic Church, denouncing it as the "mother of ignorance, superstition . . . and sin."[11]

The 1928 presidential campaign elected Republican Herbert Hoover, a dry Protestant. During the campaign, Cannon publicly assailed the religious beliefs of Hoover's Democratic opponent, Al Smith, a wet Catholic, with a viciousness that appalled many Americans, even though prejudice against Catholics was common at the time. Soon after the election, a series of embarrassing scandals involving the ASL leader, including revelations of questionable financial dealings and an extramarital affair, received wide coverage in the press. Whether or not it was fair, the League's reputation suffered along with the Bishop's. Wets had long jeered that many Prohibitionists were hypocrites, and the revelations about Cannon's financial and sexual indiscretions seemed to lend credibility to their accusations.

HERBERT HOOVER, FRANKLIN ROOSEVELT, AND "THE NOBLE EXPERIMENT"

In the November 1928 presidential election, the victory of staunch Prohibition supporter, Herbert Hoover over wet Al Smith had given new confidence to the beleaguered drys. Yet most historians agree that the Republican politician's dry stance probably had little to do with his landslide win. Given the unprecedented economic prosperity the United States had enjoyed under Hoover's Republican predecessors in the White House, Warren Harding (1921–1923) and Calvin Coolidge (1923–1929), scholars argue that Hoover, who served in both presidents' cabinets, was all but unbeatable in 1928.

In response to growing public doubts about Prohibition, during the 1928 campaign Hoover had promised to form a special panel to investigate and make recommendations about what the firm teetotaler admiringly described as America's "great social and economic experiment, noble in motive and far reaching in purpose."[12] True to his word, soon after assuming office in early 1929, President Hoover established the National Commission on Law Observance and Enforcement, popularly known as the Wickersham Commission after its chairman, former Attorney General George Wickersham, to examine Prohibition enforcement. After a 19-month investigation, in 1931, the Commission concluded that sky-high bootlegging profits and widespread public hostility toward Prohibition had

President Franklin Delano Roosevelt is pictured here in 1933, the year Prohibition was repealed. In 1932, the economic crisis that started with the stock market crash of 1929 dominated the presidential contest between incumbent Herbert Hoover and Roosevelt. Roosevelt supported the repeal of the Eighteenth Amendment, however, and his election was one signal that Prohibition would soon come to an end.

rendered the "noble experiment" all but unenforceable. Nonetheless, to the disgust of many Americans, the panel would not recommend the repeal of the Eighteenth Amendment. Adding to the public ire over the Hoover administration's handling of Prohibition was the so-called Five and Ten Act, a harsh new enforcement statute that the president helped push through

Congress a few months before the Wickersham Commission released its findings. The new law subjected bootleg liquor buyers who refused to reveal their sources to felony prosecution and significantly stiffened penalties for Volstead Act violations, increasing the maximum prison sentence for first-time offenders to five years and the maximum fine to ten thousand dollars (hence the nickname Five and Ten Act).

Despite widespread public dissatisfaction with the chief executive's Prohibition policies, during the 1932 presidential contest between Hoover and New York's wet governor, Franklin D. Roosevelt, the country's ongoing economic crisis almost completely overshadowed the liquor issue. In light of Roosevelt's public support for repeal of the Eighteenth Amendment, however, when the Democratic candidate resoundingly defeated Hoover in November 1932, there seemed little doubt that America's noble experiment would soon be coming to an end.

Prohibition's Legacy

With the election of Franklin Roosevelt and a large, pro-repeal Democratic majority in Congress in November 1932, the fate of Prohibition was sealed. Even before Roosevelt's inauguration on March 4, 1933, Congress submitted a proposed Twenty-First Amendment to the states that repealed the Eighteenth Amendment. To ensure popular control of the ratification process, the proposed amendment specified that specially called state conventions rather than state legislatures would be responsible for deciding the repeal issue. In mid-March while the states were beginning the process of electing convention delegates, at the behest of President Roosevelt, Congress passed the Beer and Wine Revenue Act that legalized the sale of light wine and beer of 3.2 percent alcoholic content or less.

Throughout the summer and autumn of 1933, the extent of the American public's disillusionment with Prohibition became evident as one state convention after another quickly ratified the Twenty-First Amendment, most by substantial majorities. On December 5, 1933, at approximately 5:30 P.M., Utah became the thirty-sixth state to approve the Twenty-First Amendment, securing the three-quarters majority required for ratification. This date marked a milestone in the history of the United States; it was the first time a constitutional amendment had ever been repealed. Indeed, as of the early twenty-first century, the Eighteenth Amendment remains the only U.S. amendment to have that dubious distinction.

The demise of national Prohibition meant that state and local governments were once again responsible for regulating alcohol. Not all Americans were prepared to go wet in 1933, however. In the immediate aftermath of repeal, a number of counties and towns, particularly in the South and Midwest, voted to remain dry, and seven states opted to prohibit the sale of hard liquor. By the end of the 1930s, however, that number had dwindled to just three: Kansas, Oklahoma, and Mississippi. Kansas would remain dry until 1948, and Oklahoma finally rescinded all of its state prohibitory laws in 1957, with Mississippi following suit nearly a decade later in 1966.

PROHIBITION'S CONSEQUENCES: THE END OF THE SALOON AND THE RISE OF NEW DRINKING NORMS

One of the most clear-cut legacies of the Prohibition Era was the death of the old-time saloon and the macho drinking culture that it had encouraged. Despite the vital role the rowdy corner saloons with their overwhelmingly male, working-class clientele had played in late nineteenth and early twentieth century urban life, they never made a comeback following repeal. "The nightclubs, cafes, bars and restaurants in which Americans drank after prohibition were not simply saloons with new names but elements of a new culture of entertainment which differed from the saloon-centered nineteenth-century world of drinking," notes Thomas Pegram.[1] Post-Prohibition bars and nightclubs, like the speakeasies of the Volstead era, emphasized social contact between the sexes and catered to younger middle- and upper-class women and men. Eager to surround their products with "an aura of glamour, wealth, and sophistication" and dissociate them from the rough image of most pre-1920 watering holes, brewers and distillers made no effort to resurrect the old-time saloon after 1933; instead, they welcomed America's new drinking patterns enthusiastically.[2]

Another transformation in American drinking habits that had its roots in the nation's "noble experiment" was the new popularity of drinking at home. During the Volstead years, fear of prosecution spurred unprecedented numbers of Americans from every social and economic class to drink in the privacy of their own homes or those of friends and acquaintances. The rise of the cocktail party, as well as the cocktail itself, dates to the Prohibition Era, when middle- and upper-class wets mixed their bootleg booze with fruit juices or soft drinks in an attempt to mask the liquor's often disagreeable or watered-down taste. Working-class drinkers also fell into the habit of drinking at home during Prohibition. The greater affordability and availability of electric refrigerators from the late 1930s on made it that much easier for laborers to enjoy their beverage of choice—cold beer—in the comfort of their homes. This also helped ensure that the new working-class drinking norms would continue long beyond repeal.

Most scholars agree that, by turning the home into a prime drinking site, Prohibition played a central role in what social scientists refer to as the normalization of drinking: the breakdown of long-held cultural taboos against liquor among the nation's Protestant Anglo-Saxon majority. The trend toward drinking at home or in upscale nightclubs or bars, as opposed to in saloons, accomplished a great deal toward the normalization of drinking in the United States because it meant that alcohol consumption was now occurring primarily in a "respectable and acceptable, non-deviant setting," maintains John Burnham.[3]

People enjoy legal drinking as they gather in New York City on December 5, 1933, after the Twenty-first Amendment was ratified. The Twenty-first Amendment repealed the Eighteenth, thereby ending Prohibition.

OTHER RESULTS: THE GROWTH OF ORGANIZED CRIME AND THE BIRTH OF AA

Although organized crime existed in urban America long before the Volstead Act, there is no question that Prohibition significantly accelerated its expansion and modernization. "The onset of Prohibition in 1920," contends author Jack Kelly, "marked the continental divide in the history of organized crime." The noble experiment "served as the gangsters' higher education, demanding as it did management skills, cooperation, planning, and high-level political contacts," he maintains: "It moved the gangs far beyond their neighborhood haunts . . . and turned street thugs into millionaires."[4] Using experience and profits gleaned from their bootlegging enterprises, once the Volstead era ended, mobsters quickly moved onto lucrative new operations, such as the illegal drug trade or protection rackets, involving a wide range of urban businesses from restaurants to limousine services.

Another very different legacy of Prohibition was the creation of the most influential self-help organization for alcohol abusers in American history, Alcoholics Anonymous (AA). During Prohibition, problem drinkers had few places to turn to for assistance: Most of the self-help organizations and so-called inebriety asylums of the pre-Volstead days disappeared after January 1920. After repeal two recovering alcoholics, William Wilson and Robert Smith, decided the time was ripe to found a new kind of self-help group, an organization whose teachings and aims would stand in stark contrast to what they viewed as the Prohibitionists' deeply flawed approach to drinking.

Strenuously rejecting the Prohibitionist assumption that all drinkers were potential alcoholics, the AA instead "drew a rigid line between normal drinkers, who could keep their consumption within the limits of moderation, and compulsive drinkers, who could not."[5] The Prohibitionist tenet that everyone was susceptible to addiction seemed to imply that those who ended up abusing liquor had less willpower than those who did not. In direct response to this demoralizing attitude, Alcoholics Anonymous insisted that alcoholism sprang from biological rather than moral causes and therefore must be treated as an illness, not a character flaw.

PROHIBITION'S REPUTATION AND CONTINUING INFLUENCE

"Perhaps the most powerful legacy of National Prohibition," writes Blocker, "is the widely held belief that it did not work."[6] According to this view, illegal drinking was so rampant

A crowd gathers as kegs of beer are unloaded in front of a restaurant on Broadway in New York City on the morning of April 7, 1933. Though Prohibition was not fully repealed until December of that year, in April Congress passed the so-called Beer Act, which permitted the manufacture of beverages containing no more than 3.2 percent alcohol.

during the Volstead era that Americans actually consumed more alcohol per capita between 1920 and 1933 than they had before Prohibition was enacted. Over the decades since repeal, the popular perception of national Prohibition as a miserable failure has been used frequently and effectively by opponents of other forms of governmental prohibition, such as of tobacco or guns. Supporters of the legalization of marijuana and other illegal drugs have tried with considerably less success to discredit narcotics laws by branding such legislation as "neo-prohibitionist," a loaded term clearly meant to conjure up images of self-righteous and narrow-minded authorities fruitlessly trying to force teetotalism on a rebellious American public.

Yet the question remains: Is the overwhelmingly negative popular judgment regarding Prohibition fair—was the noble experiment really a total flop? In recent years, a number of scholars have argued that, measured by its effect on per-capita

CANDY LIGHTNER AND MOTHERS AGAINST DRUNK DRIVERS

Early on the afternoon of Saturday, May 3, 1980, Cari Lightner, a gregarious and athletic 13-year-old, was walking along the shoulder of a quiet residential road near her California home when she was struck from behind by a speeding car that never stopped. Hurtled more than 100 feet (30.48 meters) by the impact, Cari died almost instantly. The driver was Clarence Busch, an admitted alcoholic on a three-day drinking binge. Busch, who had three prior convictions for drunk driving, was out of prison on bail for another hit-and-run accident. In 1980, the drunk driving laws in the United States were so lenient that Busch possessed a completely valid California driver's license and had never spent more than 48 hours in jail.

Cari's 34-year-old divorced mother, Candy Lightner, was devastated by her daughter's death. After learning about Busch's past, however, her grief turned to anger and a grim determination to strengthen her country's appallingly lax drunk-driving laws. Lightner quit her real estate job to devote herself to a new grassroots organization that she cofounded with Cindi Lamb, the mother of another young drunk-driving victim. Named Mothers Against Drunk Driving (MADD), the

alcohol consumption, Prohibition was far from an unmitigated failure. Although "any illegal activity is hard to measure, and prohibition violation is no exception," as David Kyvic notes, the evidence indicates that overall consumption of alcoholic beverages in the United States declined by anywhere from 33 percent to as much as 60 percent under Prohibition.[7] Moreover, for nearly four decades following repeal, per-capita annual consumption of pure alcohol among the drinking age population remained below pre-Prohibition levels of 2.5 gallons

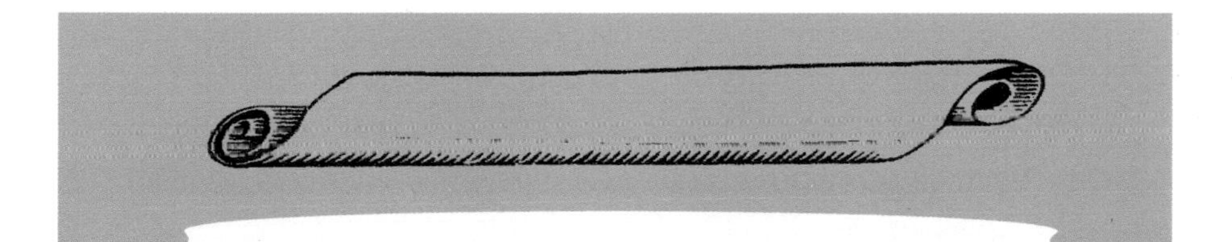

organization sought to reduce alcohol-related driving accidents in the United States by persuading state legislatures and Congress to enact harsher penalties for drunk driving and educating the public about the dangers of driving inebriated. Although Clarence Busch was convicted of vehicular homicide in Cari's death, to Lightner's disgust, the 47-year-old was sentenced to just two years in jail, of which he only served 11 months, part in a halfway house and part in a work camp.

Today, the organization that Candy Lightner helped found boasts more than 3 million members. MADD's numerous achievements include securing more severe penalties for drunk drivers, as well as persuading Congress to raise the national legal drinking age to 21 and lower the blood alcohol level at which a motorist is considered legally drunk to 0.08. In 1980, approximately 28,000 people died in alcohol-related car accidents in the United States, but the number decreased to 18,000 in 2006. Although that number is still shockingly high, according to many commentators the sharp decline in American drunk-driving fatalities since 1980 can be largely credited to the public education programs and tireless lobbying efforts of Mother's Against Drunk Drivers.

Candy Lightner (third from left), cofounder and president of Mother Against Drunk Drivers (MADD), faces reporters on June 14, 1983, on Capitol Hill in Washington, D.C. Lightner is joined by Senator Richard Lugar and Transportation Secretary Elizabeth Dole. The three favored a national drinking age of 21.

(9.46 liters). To Jack Blocker, the fact that alcohol consumption rates did not reach pre-1920 levels until 1970 suggests that, despite popular depictions of Prohibition as a complete bust, the noble experiment actually enjoyed considerable success "in socializing Americans in temperate habits."[8]

Today, annual per-capita consumption of pure alcohol in the United States is 2.8 gallons (10.60 liters), the highest rate since the early 1840s. When alcohol consumption climbed to 2.7 gallons (10.22 liters) between 1978 and 1982, concerns about binge drinking, particularly on college campuses, and driving under the influence spurred the adoption of new national alcohol regulatory laws for the first time since the repeal of the Eighteenth Amendment. In response to studies linking a higher minimum drinking age to lower alcohol-related traffic fatalities, Congress directed the states in 1984 to raise their legal age for purchasing and public possessing alcohol from 18 to 21 years or face cutbacks in federal aid highway funds. As a further measure to reduce alcohol-related traffic deaths, Congress approved legislation in 2000 that mandated a 0.08 blood alcohol concentration (BAC) as the national criterion for drunk driving, a significantly stricter BAC standard than most states used.

Recent national legislation mandating a minimum national drinking age and blood alcohol concentration standard for drunk driving are reminiscent of the federal government's decision to restrict public access to alcohol during the Prohibition Era. As in 1917, when federal lawmakers overwhelmingly approved the Eighteenth Amendment, Congressional supporters of national drinking laws in the late twentieth and early twenty-first century have been largely motivated by a desire to protect Americans against the potentially dire consequences of high-volume or reckless drinking. Yet the possibility that the United States will experience a second Prohibition Era at some point in the future appears slim. The growing social acceptability of drinking over the last century, recent findings regarding the medical benefits of moderate alcohol consumption, and last but not least, the monumental enforcement problems that plagued the Volstead years, make it highly unlikely that national Prohibition will ever return to the United States.

Chronology

1784 Benjamin Rush publishes *An Inquiry into the Effects of Spirituous Liquors*

1851 Maine becomes the first state to prohibit the manufacture and sale of alcohol.

1869 Prohibition Party is founded.

1874 Women's Christian Temperance Union is founded.

1893 Anti-Saloon League of Ohio is launched.

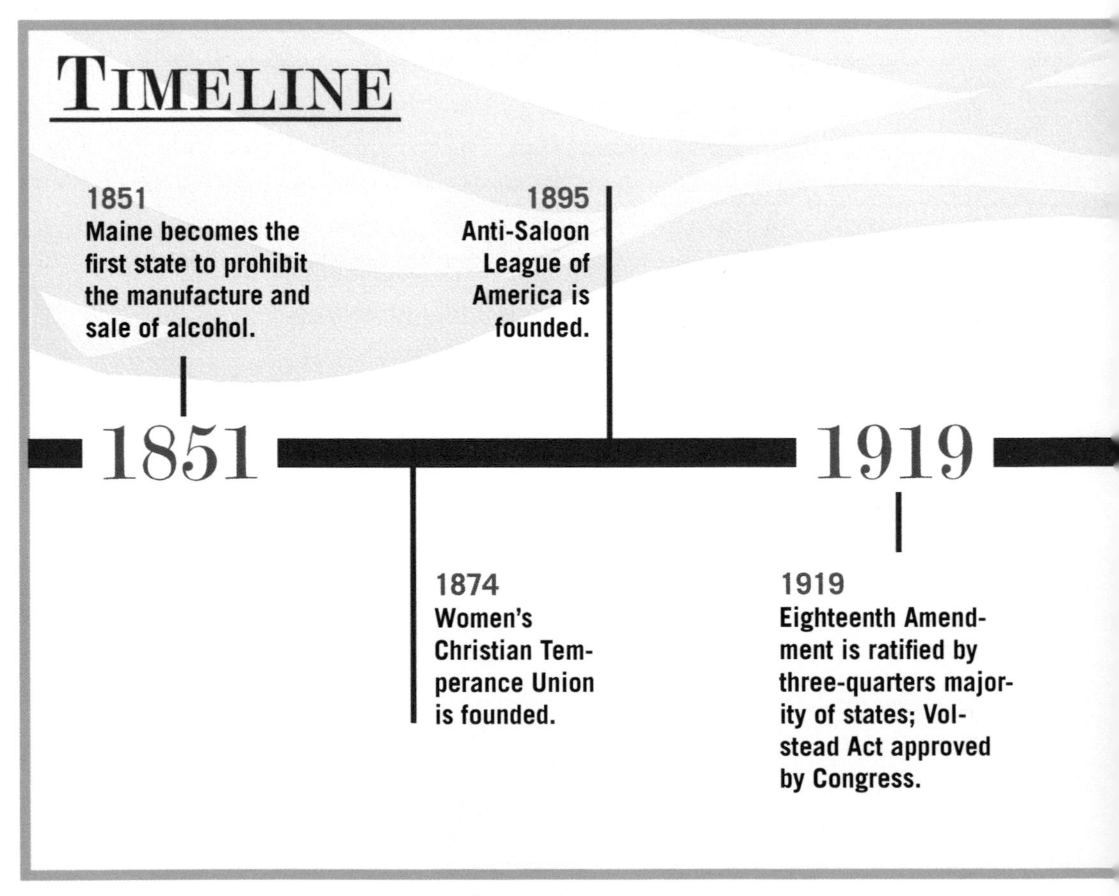

1895 Anti-Saloon League of America is founded.

1913 Webb-Kenyon Act prohibits transport of beverage alcohol into dry states.

1914 World War I begins in Europe.

1917 United States enters World War I on Allied side in April; Eighteenth Amendment passes Congress by a two-thirds majority in December.

1918 World War I ends in November.

1919 Eighteenth Amendment is ratified by three-quarters majority of states in January; Congress approves Volstead Act in October.

1920

1933

1920
The United States officially becomes a dry nation on January 17.

1929
Women's Organization for National Prohibition Reform is founded; Stock market crashes on October 29.

1933
Twenty-First Amendment, which repeals the Eighteenth Amendment, is ratified.

1920 The United States officially becomes a dry nation on January 17; Women receive the vote with the passage of the Nineteenth Amendment in August; Warren G. Harding is elected president in November.

1923 Harding dies and Calvin Coolidge becomes president.

1925 Al Capone takes over Johnny Torrio's Chicago bootlegging operation.

1928 Herbert Hoover is elected president.

1929 Valentine's Day Massacre takes place in Chicago on February 14; Women's Organization for National Prohibition Reform is founded in May; Stock market crashes on October 29.

1932 Franklin Roosevelt is elected president.

1933 Congress modifies the Volstead Act to allow sale of light beer and wine in March; Twenty-First Amendment is ratified by majority of states in December.

NOTES

CHAPTER 2

1. Mark E. Lender and James K. Martin, *Drinking in America: A History*. New York: Macmillan, 1982, p. 2.
2. Quoted in Lender and Martin, *Drinking in America*, p. 16.
3. John Kobler, *Ardent Spirits: The Rise and Fall of Prohibition*. New York: G.P. Putnam's Sons, 1973, p. 26.
4. Quoted in Kobler, *Ardent Spirits*, p. 43.
5. Quoted in Thomas R. Pegram, *Battling Demon Rum: The Struggle for a Dry America, 1800–1933*. Chicago: Ivan R. Dee, 1998, p. 14.
6. Ibid., p. 18.
7. Quoted in Sydney E. Ahlstrom, *A Religious History of the American People*. New Haven: Yale University Press, 1972, p. 646.
8. Quoted in Edward Behr, *Prohibition: Thirteen Years that Changed America*. New York: Arcade, 1996, p. 27.

CHAPTER 3

1. Quoted in Pegram, *Battling Demon Rum*, p. 70.
2. Quoted in Eric Burns, *The Spirits of America: A Social History of Alcohol*. Philadelphia: Temple University Press, 2004, p. 149.
3. Pegram, *Battling Demon Rum*, p. 117.
4. Behr, *Prohibition*, p. 50.
5. Michael A. Lerner, *Dry Manhattan: Prohibition in New York City*. Cambridge, Mass.: Harvard University Press, 2007, p. 105.
6. Burns, *The Spirits of America*, p. 151.
7. Kobler, *Ardent Spirits*, p. 194.
8. Lender and Martin, *Drinking in America*, p. 127.
9. Burns, *The Spirits of America*, p. 152.
10. Quoted in Kobler, *Ardent Spirits*, p. 183.
11. Quoted in Lender and Martin, *Drinking in America*, p. 98.

CHAPTER 4

1. Quoted in Kobler, *Ardent Spirits*, p. 198.
2. Ibid., p. 200.
3. Lender and Martin, *Drinking in America*, p. 128.
4. Quoted in Kobler, *Ardent Spirits*, p. 202.
5. J. Austin Kerr, *Organized for Prohibition: A New History of the Anti-Saloon League*. New Haven: Yale University Press, 1985, p. 160.
6. Quoted in Burns, *The Spirits of America*, p. 180.
7. Quoted in Pegram, *Battling Demon Rum*, p. 146 and Michael A. Lerner, *Dry Manhattan: Prohibition in New York City*. Cambridge, Mass.: Harvard University Press, 2007, p. 29.
8. Lender and Martin, *Drinking in America*, p. 130.

CHAPTER 5

1. Quoted in Behr, *Prohibition*, pp. 82–83.
2. David E. Kyvig, *Daily Life in the United States: 1920–1940.* Chicago: Ivan R. Dee, 2004, pp. 21–22.
3. Ibid., p. 23.
4. Burns, *The Spirits of America*, p. 191.
5. Quoted in Kobler, *Ardent Spirits*, p. 239.
6. Kobler, *Ardent Spirits*, p. 238.
7. Quoted in Behr, *Prohibition*, p. 85.
8. Kobler, *Ardent Spirits*, p. 240.
9. Quoted in Kobler, *Ardent Spirits*, p. 241.
10. Quoted in Lerner, *Dry Manhattan*, pp. 108–109.
11. Lerner, *Dry Manhattan*, pp. 173, 176.
12. Quoted in American Heritage, ed., *The American Heritage History of the 1920s and 1930s.* New York: American Heritage, 1970, p. 170.

CHAPTER 6

1. Quoted in Kobler, *Ardent Spirits*, p. 317.
2. Behr, *Prohibition*, p. 97.
3. Paul R. Kavieff, *The Purple Gang: Organized Crime in Detroit 1910–1945.* Fort Lee, N.J.: Barricade, 2005, p. 31.
4. Burns, *The Spirits of America*, pp. 216–217.
5. Quoted in Kobler, *Ardent Spirits*, p. 260.
6. Kobler, *Ardent Spirits*, p. 257.

CHAPTER 7

1. Quoted in Behr, *Prohibition*, p. 233.
2. John C. Burnham, *Bad Habits: Drinking, Smoking, Taking Drugs, Gambling, Sexual Misbehavior, and Swearing in American History.* New York: New York University Press, 1993, pp. 32–33.
3. Ibid., p. 35.
4. Kyvic, *Daily Life in the United States*, p. 24.
5. Quoted in Burnham, *Bad Habits*, p. 37.
6. Pegram, *Battling Demon Rum*, p. 159.
7. Quoted in Kobler, *Ardent Spirits*, pp. 272–273.
8. Quoted in Burns, *The Spirits of America*, p. 261.
9. Quoted in Kobler, *Ardent Spirits*, p. 343.
10. Behr, *Prohibition*, p. 229.
11. Quoted in Kobler, *Ardent Spirits*, p. 340.
12. Quoted in Lerner, *Dry Manhattan*, p. 2.

CHAPTER 8

1. Pegram, *Battling Demon Rum*, p.163.
2. John S. Blocker, Jr., "Did Prohibition Really Work? Alcohol Prohibition as a Public Health Innovation," *American Journal of Public Health.* (February 2006): p. 241.
3. Burnham, *Bad Habits*, p. 73.
4. Jack Kelly, "How America Met the Mob," *American Heritage.* (July 2000): p.76.
5. Blocker, "Did Prohibition Really Work?" p. 241.
6. Ibid., p. 241.
7. Kyvic, *Daily Life in the United States*, p. 24.
8. Blocker, "Did Prohibition Really Work?" p. 240.

Bibliography

Allen, Frederick Lewis. *Only Yesterday: An Informal History of the 1920's.* New York: Harper & Row, 1931.

American Heritage, ed. *The American Heritage History of the 1920s and 1930s.* New York: American Heritage, 1970.

Behr, Edwards. *Prohibition: Thirteen Years that Changed America.* New York: Arcade, 1996.

Blocker, Jack S. Jr. "Did Prohibition Really Work? Alcohol Prohibition as a Public Health Innovation." *American Journal of Public Health* (February 2006): pp. 233–243.

Burnham, John C. *Bad Habits: Drinking, Smoking, Taking Drugs, Gambling, Sexual Misbehavior, and Swearing in American History.* New York: New York University Press, 1993.

Burns, Eric. *The Spirits of America: A Social History of Alcohol.* Philadelphia: Temple University Press, 2004.

Coffey, Thomas M. *The Long Thirst, Prohibition in America: 1920–1933.* New York: W.W. Norton, 1975.

Kavieff, Paul R. *The Purple Gang: Organized Crime in Detroit 1910–1945.* Fort Lee, N.J.: Barricade, 2005.

Kelly, Jack. "How America Met the Mob." *American Heritage* (July 2000): pp. 76–78.

Kerr, K. Austin. *Organized for Prohibition: A New History of the Anti-Saloon League.* New Haven: Yale University Press, 1985.

Kobler, John. *Ardent Spirits: The Rise and Fall of Prohibition.* New York: G.P. Putnam's Sons, 1973.

Kyvig, David E. *Daily Life in the United States: 1920–1940.* Chicago: Ivan R. Dee, 2004.

Lender, Mark E. and James K. Martin. *Drinking in America: A History.* New York: Macmillan, 1982.

Lerner, Michael A. *Dry Manhattan: Prohibition in New York City.* Cambridge, Mass.: Harvard University Press, 2007.

Pegram, Thomas R. *Battling Demon Rum: The Struggle for a Dry America, 1800–1933.* Chicago: Ivan R. Dee, 1998.

Streissguth, Tom. *The Roaring Twenties.* New York: Facts on File, 2001.

Time Life, ed. *This Fabulous Century: 1920–1930.* Alexandria, Va.: Time-Life Books, 1969.

Further Reading

Altman, Linda Jacobs. *The Decade that Roared: America During Prohibition.* New York: Twenty-First Century, 1997.

Cohen, Daniel. *Prohibition: America Makes Alcohol Illegal.* Brookfield, Conn.: Millbrook, 1995.

Hill, Jeff. *Prohibition.* Detroit: Omnigraphics, 2004.

Nishi, Dennis, ed. *Prohibition.* San Diego: Greenhaven, 2004.

Woog, Adam, *Prohibition.* San Diego: Lucent, 2003.

Wukovits, John F., ed. *The 1920s.* San Diego: Greenhaven, 2000.

Yancey, Diane. *Al Capone.* San Diego: Lucent, 2003.

WEB SITES

About Prohibition

http://history1900s.about.com/od/1920s/p/prohibition.htm

Al Capone Biography

http://www.chicagohs.org/history/capone.html

The Anti-Saloon League

http://www.westervillelibrary.org/AntiSaloon/index.html

Carry A. Nation: The Famous and Original Bar Room Smasher

http://www.kshs.org/exhibits/carry/carry1.htm

Temperance and Prohibition

http://prohibition.osu.edu//default.cfm

Photo Credits

PAGE

3: Library of Congress, cph 3b07410
4: Library of Congress, cph 3b41628
11: The Antiquarian Society
21: AP Images
23: Library of Congress, cph 3c11068
26: Library of Congress, cph 3a16876
33: Getty Images
39: Library of Congress, cph 3b20304
53: Library of Congress, cph 3b42135
59: Getty Images
63: Library of Congress, cph 3b44030
68: © Bettmann/Corbis
72: © Bettmann/Corbis
79: AP Images
86: AP Images
89: Library of Congress, cph 3c31567
94: Library of Congress, cph 3c17121
99: AP Images
101: AP Images
104: AP Images/J. Scott Applewhite

INDEX

About the Author

LOUISE CHIPLEY SLAVICEK received her master's degree in history from the University of Connecticut. She is the author of numerous periodical articles on historical topics and 20 other books for young people, including *Women of the American Revolution*, *Israel*, and *Mother Teresa: Caring for the World's Poor.* She lives in Ohio with her husband, James, a research biologist, and their two children, Krista and Nathan.